Maximizing Effectiveness
of Reading Comprehension
Instruction in Diverse Classrooms

Maximizing Effectiveness of Reading Comprehension Instruction in Diverse Classrooms

by

Sheri Berkeley, Ph.D.
George Mason University

and

Ana Taboada Barber, Ph.D.
University of Maryland

Baltimore • London • Sydney

Paul H. Brookes Publishing Co.
Post Office Box 10624
Baltimore, Maryland 21285-0624

www.brookespublishing.com

Typeset by Scribe, Inc., Philadelphia, Pennsylvania.
Manufactured in the United States of America by
Sheridan Books, Inc., Chelsea, Michigan.

Cover images are © istockphotos/Monkeybusinessimages/MikeCherim/DragonImages/fotostorm.

Selected clip art is © 2014 Jupiterimages Corporation.

Library of Congress Cataloging-in-Publication Data

The Library of Congress has cataloged the printed edition as follows:
  Berkeley, Sheri.
  Maximizing effectiveness of reading comprehension instruction in diverse classrooms : reading strategies for diverse classrooms / Sheri Berkeley, Ph.D. and Ana Taboada Barber, Ph.D., George Mason University
  pages   cm
  Summary: "Comprehension is the ultimate goal of reading. In order for students to read and gain new understanding from texts, teachers must fully understand how to teach comprehension to a variety of learners. This supplemental textbook brings together a broad body of research on reading comprehension instruction for special education middle school and high school students in inclusive classrooms. It serves as a resource for classroom teachers as well as a practical, foundational supplemental text for undergraduate and master's level licensure programs. With its clear, research-based and applied instructional information, it will stand out in the marketplace as a text for novice teachers, both in-service and preservice. Chapters focus on a range of topics including helping students acquire new vocabulary, activating prior knowledge to make connections, utilizing reading comprehension strategies, asking questions while reading, and monitoring comprehension. By including vignettes, teaching materials, and activities, this book is an accessible, teacher-friendly volume that illustrates the most critical concepts for improving students' reading"
  ISBN 978-1-59857-306-0 (paperback)
  ISBN 978-1-59857-797-6 (EPUB)
  1. Reading comprehension. 2. Language arts (Middle school) 3. Language arts (Secondary) 4. Children with disabilities—Education. 5. Special education. 6. Inclusive education. I. Taboada Barber, Ana. II. Title.

  LB1050.45.B47 2014
  372.47—dc23   2014018511

British Library Cataloguing in Publication data are available from the British Library.

2018   2017   2016   2015   2014

10   9   8   7   6   5   4   3   2   1

Contents

About the Authors

Sheri Berkeley, Ph.D., Associate Professor, Division of Special Education and disAbility Research, George Mason University, 212 Finley Hall, MSN 1F2, Fairfax, VA 22030

Prior to her current position, Dr. Berkeley was an assistant professor at the University of Georgia and served in a diverse public school district as a special education teacher working with high-incidence populations, in both self-contained and inclusive settings, at preschool through secondary levels. Her professional efforts have aimed to improve reading outcomes for older students with learning disabilities in reading. In 2008, she received the Award for Outstanding Doctoral Level Research from the Division of Learning Disabilities in the Council for Exceptional Children for her dissertation research on reading comprehension strategy instruction for secondary students with learning disabilities. Her research has been published in numerous research journals, including *Exceptional Children, The Journal of Learning Disabilities, The Journal of Special Education, Learning Disability Quarterly,* and *Remedial and Special Education.*

Ana Taboada Barber, Ph.D., Associate Professor, Counseling, Higher Education, and Special Education, University of Maryland, 3119 Benjamin Building, College Park, MD 20742

Dr. Taboada Barber's research focuses on the examination of classroom contexts that support reading engagement for monolingual and second language learners. She is specifically interested in the psychology of literacy from a cognitive and motivational perspective. She worked on the development of the modeling of reading engagement as it applies to all learners (e.g., native speakers of English and second language learners) in the late elementary grades. She is currently working on the development of frameworks within the engagement model as they apply to second language learners. Her research has been published in the *Journal of Educational Psychology, Reading and Writing: An Interdisciplinary Journal; Journal of Literacy Research; Journal of Experimental Education; Instructional Science; Journal of*

Educational Research; and *Lectura y Vida: Latin American Journal of the International Reading Association.* She obtained her bachelor's degree in school psychology in Buenos Aires, Argentina; a master's degree in educational psychology at Temple University; and her doctoral degree from the University of Maryland. She was also a classroom teacher in bilingual schools in Buenos Aires before coming to the United States as a Fulbright scholar.

Acknowledgments

We would like to acknowledge Melissa Gallagher, Leigh Ann Kurz, and Patricia Smith for sharing their classroom experiences and expertise, which helped us create a book that is both useful and practical for teachers. We would also like to express our appreciation to them for their valuable assistance with researching, formatting, and other editorial tasks throughout the development of the manuscript. In addition, we would like to thank Kelly Liu for sharing her classroom experiences and materials.

*To Margo, Tom, and Laurie—I am forever
grateful for everything that I have learned from you*

*To John, whose mentoring opened
doors I had not envisioned before*

Maximizing Effectiveness of Reading Comprehension Instruction in Diverse Classrooms

What Is Comprehension?

Mr. Bloom asks his ninth-grade world history class to get out their textbooks. "This week we will be learning about ancient Greece, which is covered in Chapter 4 of your textbook. There will be a quiz at the end of the week, so be sure to answer the questions at the end of the chapter. You have the next 20 minutes to get started." Mr. Bloom watches as students turn to Chapter 4 and begin reading. Students sit quietly for the next 20 minutes, occasionally turning a page, and some take notes while they read.

Imagine you are Mr. Bloom. Who are the good readers? Which students are struggling to understand? It is impossible to know because reading comprehension is an internal cognitive process. Just because a student is looking in the direction of the text does not mean that he or she is understanding or even correctly identifying the words. In a typical classroom there are good readers who understand quite a bit of what they are reading and there are those who do not.

We also know that in this instance, Mr. Bloom has not provided much support to the weaker readers in his class. He is not alone—assignments like the one previously described are common in the secondary grades. There is an expectation that students will independently read to learn new information. Yet, Mr. Bloom can implement many specific practices to ensure that all students in his class are successful with these independent reading tasks—from purposeful selection of class reading materials to explicit instruction that supports reading comprehension. A description of these instructional practices is the focus of this book.

OVERVIEW OF READING COMPREHENSION

The purpose of reading is to construct meaning from print (Kintsch & Kintsch, 2005; Pullen & Cash, 2011). This process requires simultaneous proficiency in numerous skills, including the basic skills needed to gain access to print (e.g., phonemic awareness, phonics, fluency), vocabulary knowledge, and reading comprehension strategies. Furthermore, reading comprehension is an active process that requires focus from the reader before, during, and after reading. Hence, reading comprehension is complex and involves many interactions between the reader and the text itself (Klingner, Vaughn, & Boardman, 2007).

There are approximately 8 million young adults between 4th and 12th grade who struggle to read on grade level. Understanding how good readers approach text provides great insight into the reasons other students struggle with reading comprehension. Good readers connect new text with past experiences and actively interpret, evaluate, and synthesize what they read (Pressley & Afflerbach, 1995). To accomplish this, good readers are more strategic than poor readers (Paris, Lipson, & Wixson, 1983). In other words, they have a plan that they systematically follow when reading text. Contrasts between good readers and poor readers at different times in the reading process are illustrated in Table 1.1. Notice the strategic nature of good readers before, during, and after reading compared with poor readers.

Differences in student reading performance become more pronounced as students progress through the grades because the texts that they are expected to read and understand become more complex and demanding. This is especially true in content area classes in which a large amount of reading is assigned from textbooks (Wiley, Griffin, & Thiede, 2005). Textbooks contain a dense amount of new concepts and terms (Mastropieri, Scruggs, & Graetz, 2003). Close inspection of textbooks has shown that they traditionally have been written well above the students' grade level and in ways that are inconsiderate for the reader (e.g., Armbruster & Nagy, 1992). Inconsiderate texts are inconsistently organized from chapter to chapter, section to section, and even paragraph to paragraph. Although some textbooks have made progress in improving continuity, they continue to have weaknesses in the supports provided for the reader. For example, newer textbooks tend to consistently contain introductions to each chapter, and headings and subheadings accurately represent the content of those sections of text; however, textbooks continue to be written at readability levels above the grade level in which they are used, contain large numbers of unclear text structures (see Chapter 6), and include comprehension questions that are primarily detail oriented (Berkeley, King-Sears, Hott, & Bradley-Black, 2014).

Narrative texts (e.g., stories, novels) generally are easier for students to navigate and understand than expository texts (e.g., textbooks); however, they become increasingly complex as students progress through the grades. Plots become more convoluted (sometimes with multiple storylines happening simultaneously) or use alternating chronology as a storytelling device. As texts become more sophisticated, so do the skills that readers need to gain access to and make sense of what they are reading. Furthermore, there are increased requirements for K–12 students to engage with a broad range of complex informational and literary texts because of the widespread adoption of the Common Core State Standards (CCSS; Coleman & Pimentel, 2012). In addition, the number of informational texts used in middle and high school dramatically increases. Even by Grade 4, students are expected to spend a large portion of time reading informational texts across subject areas (Coleman & Pimentel, 2012). Thus, there is a clear need for teachers to understand the multiple facets of comprehension instruction for all learners, especially for those who struggle with reading.

Table 1.1. Good versus poor readers: Before, during, and after reading

	Good readers	Poor readers
Before reading	Use text features (e.g., headings, illustrations) to get a sense of what they will read and help themselves set a purpose for reading Set goals and ask questions that will help them be selective in the focus of their reading Consider what they already know about the topic Observe how text is organized, which prepares them to make connections between and among concepts	Begin reading without a purpose for reading Do not consider (or do not have) background knowledge about the topic Do not recognize how text is organized and therefore do not have a plan for how to approach reading it Lack motivation or interest in reading
During reading	Read fluently (quickly and accurately) and use word identification strategies to decode unfamiliar words Use strategies, such as context clues and prior knowledge, to figure out the meaning of vocabulary and concepts Recognize and use text structures to make connections between the meanings of sentences and/or concepts Ask and answer questions while they are reading Make predictions about what will happen next and evaluate their predictions as they read further May make mental images of what they are reading to help them visualize what they read Identify the main ideas as they read to determine what is important, what is supportive, and what is less important Monitor their reading by recognizing comprehension problems and using fix-up strategies to repair their understanding	Have difficulty decoding words, particularly multisyllable words, resulting in slow labored reading that detracts focus from comprehension. Laborious reading is also likely to result in frustration and a desire to just "get it done." Have limited vocabulary and lack strategies to figure out new words May not have background knowledge of the topic of the text, which impedes their ability to make connections between the text and what they already know Do not recognize text structures Move through the text, even if they do not understand what they have read May be easily distracted because they are not actively engaged with the text Are not aware when comprehension has broken down and/or lack strategies to repair comprehension problems when they do
After reading	Reflect on content that was read Summarize important points from the reading Draw inferences May go to other sources to clarify concepts they did not understand Believe success is a result of effort	Do not use strategies to reflect on reading Cannot summarize important points Do not seek out information to help them understand what they read Think success is a result of luck or some other external variable rather than strategic effort

HOW IS LANGUAGE DEVELOPMENT RELATED TO READING PROFICIENCY?

Although reading comprehension and writing are heavily emphasized in the secondary grades, it is important to remember that language is the foundation for all literacy skills. In some ways, these foundational skills can be thought of as the base of a pyramid that supports literacy (see Figure 1.1). If students do not have these foundational skills for understanding and using language, then they are likely to struggle with reading and writing. This is particularly true for students who have disabilities related to language (e.g., learning disability [LD], language disorder) and for those who are learning English as a second language. Following is a brief description of each of the major areas of language development—phonology, morphology, syntax, semantics, and pragmatics.

Phonology

Phonology is the study of the speech sound system of a language, including the sequences of sounds that can be combined within a language (e.g., in English we can say *daks* but not *dksa*; Moats, 2010). There are 26 letters in English that represent 44 sounds called phonemes (a phoneme is the smallest unit of sound). One letter can represent multiple sounds across words (e.g., the letter *a* in the words *ba̱t, a̱ll, a̱go,* and *ta̱ke;* the *x* in *ox̱,* which consists of both the /c/ and /s/ sounds). Alternatively, multiple letters can represent a single sound (e.g., the letters *sh* in *fi̱sẖ, ch* in *cẖaṯ,* and *oo* in *mo̱o̱t*). In addition, there are letters that are not pronounced at all (e.g., *gh* in *li̱gẖt,*

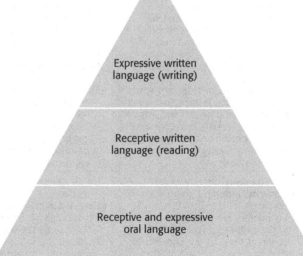

Figure 1.1. Language and literacy pyramid.

DIG DEEPER

Writing Systems

Writing systems for languages can be alphabetic or nonalphabetic. Alphabetic languages such as Spanish, French, and German use letters from the alphabet to represent sounds. Nonalphabetic languages such as Japanese and Chinese use symbols to represent sounds. English language learners (ELLs) whose first language (L1) is alphabetic will recognize letter shapes as well as some broader concepts, such as print directionality, punctuation marks, and spaces between words. Therefore, word decoding is the same process across alphabetic languages. Although the sound system may pose challenges for pronunciation and oral reading, students who are accustomed to an alphabet share basic notions of literacy, irrespective of the language.

In contrast, book orientation and print directionality will be an area of confusion for ELLs whose L1 is Chinese, Farsi, or Hebrew because these students are likely to open a book from the back cover and start reading from top to bottom. Punctuation marks or word space may be another area of difficulty for these students. In addition, because these students have never been exposed to an alphabetic writing system, it should not be surprising that they may struggle with both pronunciation and word decoding in English.

---

b in *comb; e* in *make, take,* and *case*). Although English is an alphabetic language, these examples illustrate that the mapping of sounds/phonemes to letters is not as consistent as in other alphabetic languages, such as Spanish. (See Text Box 1.1 for more information on writing systems.)

Knowledge of phonology is important to teachers of reading because phonological processing ability (the ability to notice, manipulate, and remember strings of speech sounds) explains many of the differences between students who struggle with word decoding and those who do not. Research consistently has shown that phonological skills, specifically phonemic awareness skills (the ability to manipulate phonemes), are strong predictors of later reading proficiency (Blachman et al., 2004; Wagner & Torgesen, 1987). Problems in phonemic awareness, such as segmenting and blending of individual phonemes (sounds), often result in problems with decoding, which requires students to segment and blend sounds associated with printed letters. Improving students' phonemic awareness skills alone is not sufficient, however. It is also critical to explicitly teach students how to apply the phonological skills they learn and connect letters to sounds (Foorman, Francis, Novy, & Liberman, 1991).

Morphology

Morphology consists of the study of word formation and word parts. A morpheme is the smallest unit of grammatical form that has sound and meaning

(Moats, 2010). Free morphemes can stand alone as words (e.g., elephant, house, quick), and they may have one or more syllables. Bound morphemes are meaningful units only in combination with other morphemes, including prefixes (e.g., *dis-, re-, ex-, bi-, extra-, inter-*) and suffixes (e.g., *-able, -dom, -ness, -ish, -ism, -less*). Bound morphemes never stand alone for meaning, but they need to be combined with at least one free morpheme (e.g., *-s* means more than one in the word *cats*, *re-* means to read again in the word *reread*, *-ed* means past tense in the word *escalated*).

Morphological awareness is an important aspect of language proficiency for literacy development for both monolingual and second language readers (Carlisle, 2000; Kieffer & Lesaux, 2008; Kuo & Anderson, 2006; Nagy, Berninger, & Abbott, 2006). The role that morphological awareness plays in helping students make meaning out of complex words found in academic texts is of particular importance for students in the upper elementary and secondary grades (Stahl & Nagy, 2006). For example, complex words such as *availability, likeable, projection,* and *kingdom* are more easily understood when students are made aware of word roots, suffixes, and prefixes because they can recognize the relationship to *available, like, project,* and *king* (Kieffer & Lesaux, 2012). Facilitating the learning of morphologically complex words is particularly important because these words comprise 60%–80% of the new words that school-age children must acquire to successfully read grade-level text (Anglin, 1993; Nagy & Anderson, 1984).

Syntax

Syntax refers to the underlying structure of sentences produced by speakers of a language (Moats, 2010). Syntax describes the way in which language elements (e.g., words) are put together to form larger structures (e.g., phrases, clauses). Every language has permissible word sequences that conform to the structure of the language. For example, which of the following sentences has a permissible word order in English?

• The dog chased the baker down the street.

• The dog chased down the street the baker.

The fact that we read the first sentence and think "*this sounds okay*," and we read the second sentence and think "*this does not sound right*" is an indication of our knowledge of syntax. Similarly, knowing how words should be used in relation to one another also constitutes knowledge of syntax. The English syntactic structure at its simplest level includes a subject and a predicate. The noun phrase (subject) and the verb phrase (predicate) become more complex as the basic sentence becomes more elaborate. For example, "The young red-haired girl took the apple from the dining room table" uses the basic noun (girl) and verb phrase (took the apple) structure and adds permissible words and phrases that are syntactically grouped together. Transformations—the moving of phrases to transform statements into questions, imperatives, passive voice, or from an affirmative to a negative—is another important aspect of syntax. Two examples of transformations are

1. "The dog chased the baker down the street" to "The baker was chased by the dog down the street" (active voice to passive voice).

2. "Maria does her homework every day" to "Maria does not do her homework every day" (affirmative to negative).

Transformations also follow syntactic rules and may or may not change the meaning of the original sentence, as illustrated in the previous examples.

Problems with understanding syntax may result in difficulties with reading comprehension (Stanovich, Cunningham, & Freeman, 1984). Students may struggle with the meaning or the placement of common words in the sentence, such as prepositions (e.g., in, on, below, under) and pronouns (e.g., she, him, they). For example, when reading the sentences "The nurse took good care of the patient. She made sure he was not cold by asking him, 'Would you like another blanket?'" a student might be confused about who *she, he,* and *him* refer to respectively. Cohesion (e.g., but, however, therefore) or time markers (e.g., then, next, first) can also pose challenges. These challenges become more pronounced when reading academic texts that comprise complex grammatical structures such as if-then sentences with coordinating conjunctions such as *and, but, for, nor, or, so,* and *yet.* For example, sentences such as "They may take our lives, but they will not take our freedom" or sentences with dependent clauses, such as "Dorothy lived on a farm with Uncle Berry, who was a farmer," are especially challenging because students need to not only understand the content words but also the role of the conjunctions (i.e., *but* in the first sentence) and the clause (i.e., *who was a farmer* within the second sentence).

Semantics

Semantics is the study of meaning, and more specifically, the meaning of words, word phrases, and sentences (Moats, 2010). Word meanings are arbitrary and are agreed to over time by speakers of a language. For example, there is no reason why the word *tow* means one thing and the word *town* means another. Although word meanings are agreed on by convention and are constantly evolving, speakers are not free to change meanings at will—this would make communication impossible.

Semantics can refer to the knowledge of the meanings of words, the understanding of the relationship between and among words, and the awareness that words can have shades of meaning, including multiple meanings. For example, consider the variations of the meanings for the word *scale* in the following sentences:

- The fishmonger prepared to *scale* the fish.

- The veterinarian weighed the dog on the *scale*.

- You need to *scale* back the costs of this wedding.

- The map is not to *scale*.

- Snakes and other reptiles have *scales*.

- Please get out your flute and practice your *scales*.

The word *scale* clearly does not have one meaning. Rather, this single word has numerous meanings and shades of meanings.

Semantics also can include the understanding of meaning within phrases and sentences. Although words in sentences may be syntactically correct, they can be semantically incorrect, such as in the following sentence: "Shapeless round towns learn heartily." In this example, something cannot be both shapeless and round, and towns are inanimate objects that cannot learn. Therefore, even if each individual word is known, the meaning is still lost. In addition, some word phrases, such as figurative language, cannot be interpreted literally. To illustrate, each of the following idioms contain the word *bird,* yet they cannot be understood literally.

- Free as a *bird.*

- A *bird* in the hand is worth two in the bush.

- *Birds* of a feather flock together.

- The early *bird* gets the worm.

- Kill two *birds* with one stone.

"Kill two birds with one stone" does not actually suggest that any birds should be killed, but rather that one action could solve two problems. Inference skills and knowledge of the culture are needed to correctly interpret the semantic meaning of this phrase. Semantic knowledge generally is addressed through vocabulary development and instruction. Vocabulary instruction is discussed in detail in Chapter 3.

Pragmatics

Pragmatics refers to how language is interpreted within context. Three primary communication areas are related to pragmatics: using language, changing language, and following rules of language (American Speech-Language-Hearing Association [ASHA], 2013). Language is conventionally used for greeting, informing, demanding, promising, or requesting. The ways that words are phrased convey the intention (e.g., "I am going to get a brownie" versus "Give me a brownie" versus "May I have a brownie?"). The language we use often is situational, however, so pragmatics also includes how language changes based on context. For example, a child's letter to the school principal should not have the same tone as an e-mail to his or her close friend. Finally, pragmatics includes the rules that are followed in conversation that are both verbal (e.g., turn-taking, introducing and maintaining topics) and nonverbal (e.g., knowing how close to stand when speaking, making eye contact, using appropriate facial expressions). Within the context of literacy, this is the situational context that aids in the correct interpretation of language, including written language (Moats, 2010). Social conventions related to language are important in both oral and written language, but they can vary based on situational and cultural context. For example, tone of voice in certain cultures is much more moderate than in others in which louder speaking is more socially acceptable. Understanding pragmatics can aid in the accurate interpretation of language within different contexts.

WHY DO SOME STUDENTS STRUGGLE WITH LEARNING LANGUAGE?

Today's classrooms are incredibly diverse with a wide range of different types of learners, including those who struggle with reading (Hock, Schumaker, & Deshler, 1999). Two of these populations are students with LD and students who are English language learners (ELLs). Reading disabilities (LD in the area of reading) affect 15%–20% of all children and adolescents (Hallahan, Lloyd, Kauffman, Weiss, & Martinez, 2005; Lyon, Alexander, & Yaffe, 1997; Shaywitz, 2003), and one in five students live in homes where a language other than English is spoken (International Reading Association, 2007). Therefore, it is important that teachers have a working knowledge of how to assist these students.

Students Who Have Learning Disabilities

Students with LD have average to above-average intelligence, but due to a disorder in one or more of the basic psychological processes involved in understanding and/or using language (spoken or written), are unable to listen, think, speak, read, write, spell, or do mathematical calculations, at the level expected for typically developing students of their age (Individuals with Disabilities Education Improvement Act [IDEA] of 2004, PL 108-446). (See Text Box 1.2 for more information on how students with LD are identified.) These students often display cognitive processing deficits in visual processing, auditory processing, and/or language (Jennings, Caldwell, & Lerner, 2010). In addition, they often display deficits in metacognition, social skills, attention, memory, and motor skills (Pullen, Lane, Ashworth, & Lovelace, 2011). Brain research has revealed that there are neurological and cognitive factors that vary between poor readers and those that develop typically (Shaywitz, Morris, & Shaywitz, 2008; Shaywitz & Shaywitz, 1998). These characteristics can affect many areas of learning, but particularly reading. In fact, almost 50% of students in special education have an LD, and it is estimated that 80%–90% of students with LD struggle in the area of reading (Lerner & Johns, 2009; Pullen et al., 2011).

Text Box

1.2

DIG DEEPER

Defining Learning Disabilities

In 1963, Samuel Kirk was one of the first to coin the term *learning disability* (LD; Hallahan, Lloyd, Kauffman, Weiss, & Martinez, 2005). Since then, there have been many variations of the definition of LD. The current definition within the federal law that mandates special education services for students with disabilities, the Individuals with Disabilities Education Improvement Act (IDEA) of 2004 (PL 108-446), states

> Specific learning disability means a disorder in one or more of the basic psychological processes involved in understanding or in using language, spoken or written, that may manifest itself in the imperfect ability to listen, think, speak, read, write, spell, or to do mathematical calculations, including conditions such as perceptual disabilities, brain injury, minimal brain dysfunction, dyslexia, and developmental aphasia.
>
> Specific learning disability does not include learning problems that are primarily the result of visual, hearing, or motor disabilities, of mental retardation, of emotional disturbance, or of environmental, cultural, or economic disadvantage.

LEARNING DISABILITIES OR DYSLEXIA?

Severe reading disabilities are sometimes referred to as *dyslexia* (Jennings, Caldwell, & Lerner, 2010; Pullen, Lane, Ashworth, & Lovelace, 2011). The federal definition of LD does not delineate by severity; thus, even if a student is diagnosed by a physician as having dyslexia, he or she will receive special education services under the IDEA disability category of LD. Similarly, LD in the area of handwriting is sometimes referred to as *dysgraphia,* and LD in the area of math computation and concepts is sometimes referred to as *dyscalculia.* These students would qualify for special education services under the general category of LD as well.

CURRENT TRENDS IN LEARNING DISABILITY IDENTIFICATION

A major controversy surrounding LD has been in the specific criteria used for identification of the disability. The federal criteria for identification of an individual with LD traditionally was met through testing that established a severe discrepancy between an individual's ability (generally measured by an IQ test) and his or her academic achievement (generally measured by a norm-referenced achievement test) that could not be otherwise explained. This process is referred to as the discrepancy model.

Over time, concerns were raised in the field regarding this approach to LD identification. For example, some researchers questioned the appropriateness of measuring an individual's ability solely by an IQ test (Hallahan et al., 2005). Determining the extent of discrepancy necessary for special education identification and services was also questioned because states set their own criteria, which resulted in variation in eligibility thresholds across the country (Cortiella, 2008). In addition, the discrepancy model has often been criticized as the wait to fail method that detects LD only after the child has experienced years of failure (National Center for Learning Disabilities, 2013).

In the most recent reauthorization of IDEA (2004), additional eligibility models are now permitted for LD identification.

The response to intervention (RTI) model is perhaps the most common alternative approach. RTI can be defined as both a student-centered model used to address learning difficulties (Johnson, Mellard, Fuchs, & McKnight, 2006) and an identification process for determining whether a student is eligible for special education due to an LD. RTI approaches are often referred to as tiered because students move through tiers that become increasingly more intense in both instruction and progress monitoring (starting in general education, progressing to small-group interventions, and culminating in special education if students do not respond to the intervention). Core components of RTI include high-quality general education classroom instruction (including entire class and small-group remediation), universal screening (to identify students who may be at risk), research-based interventions (that have been documented to be effective in the areas of concern), continuous progress monitoring (to evaluate how well selected interventions are working for targeted students), and fidelity of instructional interventions (to establish that the intervention was delivered as intended). Providing assistance to struggling students right away (rather than waiting for them to fail) is the intended outcome of RTI, which potentially prevents the need for many students to require special education services.

RTI is not without criticisms, however. Areas of concern include a lack of documentation of students' general cognitive ability that can result in slow learners being labeled with an LD, interventions being utilized in RTI that may not have strong empirical evidence supporting effectiveness, failure to differentiate LD from other high-incidence disabilities, and limited information about how RTI should be implemented at the secondary level (Berkeley, Bender, Peaster, & Saunders, 2009; Fuchs & Vaughn, 2012; Scruggs & Mastropieri, 2002). Many states are addressing these concerns by using a combination of RTI and formal assessment approaches in the eligibility process.

Students with LD possess the cognitive ability to process information, but they do so inefficiently (Gersten, Fuchs, Williams, & Baker, 2001), which results in an array of reading challenges that compound over time if effective interventions are not received. Students with LD often possess limited knowledge of types of text and how text is structured (Gersten et al., 2001); display inadequate vocabulary knowledge, particularly compared with peers (Jitendra, Edwards, Sacks, & Jacobson, 2004); inappropriately reference background knowledge (Williams, 1993); and have difficulty with tasks involving language and abstractions (Swanson & Hoskyn, 1998). In addition, students with LD often fail to read strategically and to monitor their understanding of what they are reading (Vaughn, Gersten, & Chard, 2000). Furthermore, students with LD are less likely to self-regulate their learning, persist with tasks, and retain what they have learned (Gersten et al., 2001). Finally, students with LD often display a lack of motivation that affects their engagement in academic tasks, including reading (Fulk, Brigham, & Lohman, 1998; Sideridis & Scanlon, 2006).

Most students with LD are taught in inclusive general education classroom settings. Specifically, 59% of students with LD spend 80% or more of the school day in general education settings (U.S. Department of Education [USDOE], 2009), and they are expected to demonstrate their learning of general curriculum content on state tests. This means that these students are expected to learn the complex content of the general curriculum at a rapid pace, despite their challenges with learning (Woodruff, Schumaker, & Deshler, 2002). Teachers need to have knowledge of a wide range of instructional approaches to help students accomplish this goal and to address the needs of all learners within the classroom. In addition, many students with LD require additional supports in language development. (See Text Box 1.3 for more information about the relationship between speech-language disorders and LD.)

Text Box

1.3

PRACTICAL APPLICATION

The Relationship Between Speech-Language Disorders and Learning Disabilities

A student's success in learning to read can be affected by underlying problems with language (Jennings, Caldwell, & Lerner, 2010).

There are two primary types of language problems for which students may receive special education services under the Individuals with Disabilities Improvement Act (IDEA) of 2004, PL 108-446—*speech disorders* and *language disorders*. There are three scenarios where students can receive services for speech-language disorders:

1. As a *primary disability* under IDEA (e.g., speech-language disorder)

2. As a *secondary disability* under IDEA (e.g., the student's primary disability is a learning disability [LD], and a secondary disability is a speech-language disorder)

3. As a *related service* similar to other related services, such as occupational or physical therapy (e.g., the student's primary disability is an LD, and the student also receives related services for a speech-language disorder)

Approximately half of the students who receive speech-language services are identified as having a speech-language disorder as a primary disability; the other half receive services due to a secondary disability or as a related service (Power de-Fur, 2011).

SPEECH DISORDERS

A speech disorder occurs when an individual does not correctly produce speech sounds or with fluency (American Speech-Language-Hearing Association [ASHA], 2005). Examples of speech disorders include difficulty with articulation (problems producing sounds when speaking) and stuttering. Speech impairments can impede a student's performance on reading assessments that require students to read aloud. For example, if a student omits the /-s/ from the endings of words when speaking (e.g., the student says *cat* instead of *cats*), then the student will do so when reading aloud as well. It is important in such a scenario that the student not be penalized in the scoring of the assessment because this will deflate the student's overall score and underestimate the student's true abilities. It is important, however, to be thoughtful regarding which errors are not penalized. For example, the same student may leave many endings off of words while reading (e.g., *-ed, -ing, -er*), even though /s/ is the only sound that he or she cannot articulate. In this case, these additional word ending miscues should be counted as errors so that these sounds are targeted within reading instruction. How can a teacher verify whether the issue is reading related or speech related? After the student reads a passage, the teacher can ask the student to repeat aloud words that have the same endings that were questionable in text. If the student can correctly repeat the word, then it is likely a reading error. If the student cannot correctly repeat the word, then it is likely an articulation error.

LANGUAGE DISORDERS

Language disorders are difficulties with receptive language (understanding what is heard) and/or expressive language (conveying ideas, thoughts, or feelings with others; ASHA, 2005). Because language is at the heart of reading and writing, a language disability can greatly affect a student's academic performance. Children with language disorders have particular difficulty developing the language skills described in this chapter. In addition, children with language disorders may experience difficulty in reading and comprehension as well as understanding others, communicating thoughts, and solving problems (ASHA, 2005). Instructional approaches for addressing areas of difficulty related to reading (and underlying language problems) are the focus of the remaining chapters.

Students Who Are English Language Learners

ELLs are students born both within and outside of the United States who speak a language other than English at home and whose English proficiency is not yet developed, limiting their ability to learn grade-level academic material in English (August & Shanahan, 2006). Developing foundational language skills is one of the challenges to teaching reading comprehension to ELLs. (See Text Box 1.4 for language development issues specific to ELLs.)

Text Box

1.4

DIG DEEPER

Language Acquisition Issues
Specific to English Language Learners

Oral language is fundamental for later success in reading and writing for all students. However, teachers should be aware of additional considerations related to language development when they are working with English language learners (ELLs).

PHONOLOGY

Inconsistencies in the mapping of sounds to letters in English can be challenging for many students, but particularly those who are learning English as a second language. Because some sounds in English do not exist in the ELL's first language (L1), a student might pronounce sounds as he or she would for similar sounds in his or her L1. For example, many ELLs who speak Spanish will confuse /sh/ for /ch/, saying *chop* for *shop* and vice versa. Also, ELLs who speak Spanish are likely to struggle with letter–sound correspondences that are inconsistent in English but not in Spanish. For example, they may struggle to learn that the sound of a letter may change depending on its position in a single-syllable or a multisyllable word (e.g., how *y* is pronounced in *why* or *cry* versus in *happy* or *lucky*).

MORPHOLOGY

Teaching word roots, prefixes, and suffixes is of high importance for an ELL's reading development and cannot be overemphasized. In addition to developing morphological awareness, however, these students need to be made aware of the variations in pronunciation of word families that share the same roots, particularly when the root originates from or has the same meaning as the student's L1. For instance, consider the two different sounds in the words *cyclical* and *cycle*, which share the same root *cycl* (circle), or the two sounds in *dictionary, indict,* and *dictator,* which share the same root *dict* (speak). Pronunciation of these words varies, although they are from the same word families. Once a student recognizes these patterns, however, they can help promote decoding, spelling, and vocabulary development.

SYNTAX

Many students struggle with understanding syntax, but this is especially true for students who are learning English. ELLs are confronted not only with learning academic vocabulary, but also the academic register that is assumed in texts and the language of school because of the complexities of academic language. In addition, ELLs who speak Spanish may struggle with the word order of adjectives and nouns in English because it is the opposite in Spanish (i.e., the adjective comes before the noun in English as in "the red book," but the noun comes before the adjective in Spanish as in "el libro rojo"). For ELLs who are Asian, English articles such as *a, an,* and *the* are difficult and often omitted because they are nonexistent in many Asian languages (Barone & Xu, 2008). Last, sentence transformations, especially the use of auxiliary verbs in interrogative and negative forms (e.g., "Mary does not like hot dogs" versus "Does Mary like hot dogs?"), and the inverse word order and verb change in the passive voice can be especially challenging for ELLs. Therefore, these students need the appropriate scaffolding and explicit instruction that allows them to build academic language and the ability to communicate about content.

SEMANTICS

Words, phrases, and sentences are essential for meaning making during reading. A great emphasis is placed on teaching ELLs vocabulary, sometimes with the risk of losing track of the importance of teaching words in context (i.e., in sentences and paragraphs). The example provided earlier about the multiple meanings of the word *scale* provides a good case of why multiple meanings of the same word are better taught in the context of a sentence (see page 8). In addition, there could be meaning interferences from their L1 for some ELLs because of the different meaning of the same word across the two languages. For example, the Spanish word for *spend* is *gastar*, which includes other meanings such as to waste, use up, and, even in some versions of Spanish slang, to tease. As such, an ELL who speaks Spanish may say or write "I wasted $4 on this pencil," even when he or she does not want to convey the English meaning of to waste (Xu, 2010).

PRAGMATICS

Pragmatics is especially relevant for ELLs given the varying norms and customs that are part of spoken and written communication in different cultures. Challenges for ELLs will differ according to their varying cultural backgrounds. For example, physical approximation in spoken language in Spanish-speaking cultures is much less defined than in Anglo cultures. Similarly, higher tones are much more permissible in many Asian cultures than in others. Although many of these differences can be seen as enriching the U.S. classrooms as multicultural contexts, many students attempting to assimilate and learn the norms of school rules and academic language would likely appreciate being made aware of language pragmatics in the main culture.

The majority of ELLs in the United States speak Spanish. These students often come from poverty, have had limited education in their first language (L1), and are unlikely to have literacy skills in English or their L1. If this is the case, then these students are likely to be lacking the academic experiences needed to succeed in school. They will need English language skills as well as school experiences that will allow them to build prior knowledge on key topics in order to meet on-grade academic standards.

Other groups of ELLs, however, have a well-developed L1 literacy knowledge that can help boost their learning and reading in English. This latter group is still developing English proficiency, and many of those students may be new to schools in the United States. These students present a different set of skills that can be used to help them activate their prior knowledge. More specifically, if the child has developed literacy in his or her L1, then both the classroom and the ELL teacher have an easier road ahead than if the child is lacking these skills altogether. A child who has learned to read in his or her L1 can transfer those skills to English and is likely to have developed knowledge in a variety of domains compared with the child with limited literacy in his or her L1. In fact, studies have shown the benefits of transferring skills from an L1 to the second language (L2) for different dimensions of reading, such as vocabulary and comprehension (Carlo et al., 2004; Proctor, Carlo, August, & Snow, 2006).

ELLs come to the United States from a variety of circumstances. Some students have done most of their formal schooling in the United States, whereas others are newcomers and have done all or some prior schooling in their home country—often with great variability in the educational experiences to which they have been exposed. All children bring multiple resources to school, which vary from child to child and from those of native English speakers. These diverse experiences can be described as funds of knowledge and may include cultural practices, religious beliefs, oral storytelling, knowledge about agriculture and mining, household management, and medicine (Moll, Amanti, Neff, & González, 1992). These funds of knowledge represent a rich foundation on which to build students' development of literacy. As ELLs begin to learn an L2, their development is typically captured within levels (or stages). The World Class Instructional Design and Assessment (WIDA) levels are commonly used within schools (see Figure 1.2). Therefore, inquiring about the L2 proficiency level of the student is a starting point for the classroom teacher. Knowing typical L2 development can help the teacher understand the learning needs students may have as they are beginning to learn English. In addition, the teacher should attempt to find out as much as possible about an ELL's formal education experiences in order to determine what literacy instruction was received in the L1 and in English (if any).

Dual Diagnosis

In some cases, students may be an ELL and have an LD, but this can be challenging to determine. A question commonly raised by classroom teachers is, "Do ELLs struggle with reading because of their limited English proficiency or because they have a specific reading disability?" Many general education teachers refer ELLs to special education because they think "at least they will get some help." Others hesitate to refer ELLs who are struggling to special education because they believe they are required to wait for ELLs to learn English so that language can be ruled out as the cause of the student's difficulty (Hamayan, Marler, Sanchez-Lopez, & Damico, 2007). Both of these lines of thinking can result in overrepresentation and underrepresentation of ELLs in special education (Donovan & Cross, 2002).

For the given level of English language proficiency, **with support,** English language learners can:

	Level 1 Entering	Level 2 Beginning	Level 3 Developing	Level 4 Expanding	Level 5 Bridging	Level 6 Reaching
LISTENING	• Point to stated pictures, words, phrases • Follow one-step oral directions • Match oral statements to objects, figures or illustrations	• Sort pictures, objects according to oral instructions • Follow two-step oral directions • Match information from oral descriptions to objects, illustrations	• Locate, select, order information from oral descriptions • Follow multi-step oral directions • Categorize or sequence oral information using pictures, objects	• Compare/contrast functions, relationships from oral information • Analyze and apply oral information • Identify cause and effect from oral discourse	• Draw conclusions from oral information • Construct models based on oral discourse • Make connections from oral discourse	Level 6 Reaching
SPEAKING	• Name objects, people, pictures • Answer WH- (who, what, when, where, which) questions	• Ask WH- questions • Describe pictures, events, objects, people • Restate facts	• Formulate hypotheses, make predictions • Describe processes, procedures • Retell stories or events	• Discuss stories, issues, concepts • Give speeches, oral reports • Offer creative solutions to issues, problems	• Engage in debates • Explain phenomena, give examples and justify responses • Express and defend points of view	
READING	• Match icons and symbols to words, phrases or environmental print • Identify concepts about print and text features	• Locate and classify information • Identify facts and explicit messages • Select language patterns associated with facts	• Sequence pictures, events, processes • Identify main ideas • Use context clues to determine meaning of words	• Interpret information or data • Find details that support main ideas • Identify word families, figures of speech	• Conduct research to glean information from multiple sources • Draw conclusions from explicit and implicit text	
WRITING	• Label objects, pictures, diagrams • Draw in response to a prompt • Produce icons, symbols, words, phrases to convey messages	• Make lists • Produce drawings, phrases, short sentences, notes • Give information requested from oral or written directions	• Produce bare-bones expository or narrative texts • Compare/contrast information • Describe events, people, processes, procedures	• Summarize information from graphics or notes • Edit and revise writing • Create original ideas or detailed responses	• Apply information to new contexts • React to multiple genres and discourses • Author multiple forms/genres of writing	

Variability of students' cognitive development due to age, grade level spans, their diversity of educational experiences and diagnosed learning disabilities (if applicable) are to be considered in using this information.

Figure 1.2. Second language proficiency. (WIDA ELD Standards © 2007, 2012 Board of Regents of the University of Wisconsin System. WIDA is a trademark of the Board of Regents of the University of Wisconsin System. For more information on using the WIDA ELD Standards, please visit the WIDA web site at www.wida.us)

17

Determining if an ELL's challenges with reading are due to the language proficiency level or because of an LD can be a complex process (USDOE, 2003). Teachers are not alone in making this determination, however. A team of professionals (including parents) ultimately makes the decision about whether a student qualifies for special education services after reviewing multiple sources of information, including observations, records review, and formal testing—generally in a student's L1 and L2 if he or she is not a native English speaker. Before conducting a formal evaluation, most schools have professionals available that can assist classroom teachers in the best way to proceed—this can range from a single special education teacher to a team of professionals that provide guidance (the names of these prereferral teams vary throughout the country). The advice given generally includes recommendations for instructional strategies that teachers can use in the classroom, directions for how to monitor student progress, and/or guidance for how to collect documentation should an evaluation for special education be determined to be appropriate.

WHAT DOES THIS MEAN FOR CLASSROOM TEACHERS?

It is important that teachers differentiate instruction to meet the needs of all students, including students with LD and those who are ELLs. Therefore, in addition to knowing what to teach, teachers need to know what research tells us about *how* to teach. This book contains a wide variety of teaching strategies that are commonly used in classrooms to help students improve skill areas that are critical for reading comprehension. Each chapter includes cautions that teachers should keep in mind when working with students with

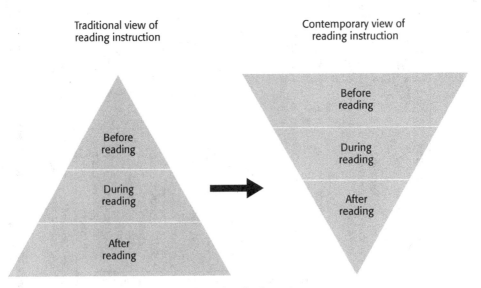

Figure 1.3. Traditional versus contemporary views of reading instruction.

particular challenges in reading, such as students with LD or ELLs. In addition, it is important to remember that supports for students should occur throughout the reading process—which includes before, during, and after reading.

In the past, the bulk of this instructional support occurred after students finished reading, much like in Mr. Bloom's class described at the beginning of the chapter. However, frontloading instruction for students who are struggling in the area of reading can be a much more effective approach. Learning strategies that happen before and during reading can help students overcome challenges that they face when gaining access to and attempting to understand text, resulting in improved comprehension (see Figure 1.3).

How have you approached instruction in your classroom? Do the bulk of your teaching efforts occur after students have finished reading? Or do you spend your instructional efforts before students begin reading so that they are prepared to gain access to and navigate the text?

2

Basic Reading Skills

Difficulty in basic reading skills such as decoding and fluency can serve as a barrier to reading comprehension for students who are not proficient in these important skills. Teachers need to understand both the basic reading abilities of their students and the demands of the text that they select for both instruction and independent reading assignments.

WHAT ARE BASIC READING SKILLS AND WHY ARE THEY IMPORTANT FOR READING?

"The ultimate goal of reading instruction at the secondary level is comprehension—gaining meaning from text" (Edmonds et al., 2009, p. 263). Yet, this outcome does not always occur. Research (e.g., Carlisle & Rice, 2002; National Reading Panel, 2000) has indicated that comprehension can break down for several reasons, including problems with basic reading skills such as decoding words (including structural analysis of multisyllable words) and fluency (i.e., reading speed, accuracy of decoding, proper inflection—called prosody). Conversely, proficiency in basic reading skills enables comprehension of text (Chard, Vaughn, & Tyler, 2002; Joseph & Schisler, 2009; Levy, Abello, & Lysynchuk, 1997). Clearly, students who have not acquired basic reading skills by middle school are at a disadvantage (Biancarosa & Snow, 2004).

It is imperative that instruction be provided to students who struggle with basic decoding skills because poorly skilled readers fall further behind their typically achieving peers over time (Judge & Bell, 2011). Yet, even excellent basic reading instruction in the early elementary grades does not guarantee that students will be successful with higher level literacy demands in the upper grades (Biancarosa, 2012). Basic reading instruction in the primary grades focuses on word reading skills such as letter–sound correspondences, blending sounds into words, and fluently reading words (Joseph & Schisler, 2009). This instruction lessens, however, beginning in the fourth grade. In essence, students are expected to "learn to read" in the early grades, but beginning in fourth grade, explicit instruction in basic skills dramatically decreases and students are increasingly expected to "read to learn" (Chall, 1983). Many students are unprepared for these shifting expectations. National data indicated that only 67% of fourth graders were able to read at a proficient level (National Center for Educational Statistics, 2012). There are two major problems with this reality.

First, reading demands continue to increase after fourth grade (when basic reading instruction begins to decrease). Texts, including content area textbooks, contain varied and complex text structures (rather than basic narrative stories that students are exposed to in the primary grades). Furthermore, students are expected to read a variety of texts that become more distinct by content area (Heller & Greenleaf, 2007). Sentences become more complex and contain more unfamiliar words that are longer and more challenging to decode. In addition, the amount of text that students are expected to read and understand dramatically increases (Carnegie Council on Advancing Adolescent Literacy, 2010). Students often have no explicit instruction in how to approach these types of texts or how to approach decoding multisyllable words. In addition, students are less able to figure out unknown words from context when they are reading content for which they have no prior knowledge. (The role of prior knowledge will be further dicsussed in Chapter 4).

Second, many students do not master word reading skills by third grade, which impedes their fluency and text comprehension (Denton, Wexler, Vaughn, & Bryan, 2008). Many of these students—particularly students with learning disabilities (LD), continue to struggle with basic reading skills by the time they reach middle and high school and display the same decoding errors demonstrated by much younger children (Lovett et al., 2008). Students with LD often display slower growth rates of both decoding and fluency compared with their typically developing peers (Katz, Stone, Carlisle, Corey, & Zeng, 2008). English language learners (ELLs) may also lack proficiency in basic skills due to limited proficiency in English or arrested early literacy development (e.g., poor phonological awareness either in their first language [L1] or in English). ELLs may have had inconsistent instruction in their L1, and these students may also struggle to develop oral language proficiency in English in addition to their challenges with word-level skills. (See Text Box 2.1 for more information on the oral language proficiency and reading skills of ELLs.)

HOW ARE BASIC SKILLS TAUGHT AT THE SECONDARY LEVEL?

Students in early elementary school generally have one teacher for the entire school day and reading skills are taught primarily during language arts class. As students advance through the grades, they are taught by an increasing number of teachers who specialize in a subject area (e.g., U.S. history, biology, algebra). In addition, language arts curricula begin to shift away from basic

Text Box

2.1

DIG DEEPER

Second Language Oral Language Proficiency and Reading Skills: What the Research Says

The *Report of the National Literacy Panel on Language-Minority Children and Youth* (August & Shanahan, 2006) was an instrumental tool in summarizing research on literacy development of English language learners (ELLs). Although this comprehensive report has been written mostly for researchers, the following are a few research-based conclusions on the relationships between second language (L2) oral language proficiency and basic reading skills that will be important to teachers.

- English oral language proficiency (typically assessed as vocabulary and grammatical knowledge) is not always strongly related or predictive of students' word reading skills in English. Rather it is students' phonological awareness in their first language (L1) and/or L2 that is strongly related to reading words and pseudowords in English (Durgunoglu, Nagy, & Hancin-Bhatt, 1993; Gottardo, 2002; Quiroga, Lemos-Britton, Mostafapour, Abbot, & Berninger, 2002).

- The finding that there is a weak relationship between English oral language proficiency and word reading in English applies to ELLs of multiple language backgrounds (not only Hispanic ones). ELLs of multiple L1 backgrounds have also been found to show a strong association between phonological skills (e.g., phonological awareness, rapid naming of letters) and word reading in English (Geva, Yaghoub-Zadeh, & Schuster, 2000). However, English oral language proficiency consistently relates to ELLs' reading comprehension (Beech & Keys, 1997; Carlisle, Beeman, Davis, & Spharim, 1999; Manis, Lindsey, & Bailey, 2004; Taboada, 2012) and writing (Davis, Carlisle, & Beeman, 1999; Lanauze & Snow, 1989). ELLs who have more developed oral language skills tend to comprehend text better (Goldstein, Harris, & Klein, 1993; Lee & Schallert, 1997; Peregoy, 1989).

WHAT ARE INSTRUCTIONAL IMPLICATIONS FOR TEACHERS OF ENGLISH LANGUAGE LEARNERS?

- Development of oral language proficiency is of key importance when larger chunks of text are involved, such as comprehending sentences, paragraphs, or whole sections of text in English. Therefore, make sure ELLs receive both formal instruction in oral English as well as exposure to English via informal ways (e.g., conversations with classmates who speak English, social talk at break time, exposure to models of appropriate English usage by teachers and other adults).

- Phonological skills may not directly relate to oral English vocabulary, but they are fundamental to word decoding and reading with automaticity and fluency. Therefore, make sure ELLs have these foundational skills in place.

- Both English oral language proficiency and word reading skills require specific, explicit instruction—one does not assume the other.

reading instruction and toward understanding various literary forms. Because the content of the curriculum and the structure of the school day no longer lend themselves to explicit instruction in basic reading, students who still require basic reading instruction are often placed in a remedial reading class as one of their elective classes. These classes generally are taught by a reading specialist or a special education teacher with expertise in intensive reading instruction methods. Figure 2.1 illustrates reading programs commonly used in remedial reading classes and skills that are addressed within each program.

Students may be weak in basic reading skills in some instances, but not to the extent that an intensive reading program would be appropriate. Supplemental instruction might be provided to these students through technology (often referred to as *computer-assisted instruction* [CAI]). Numerous software programs on the market can be used to help teachers differentiate instruction in basic reading skills. Technology allows practice to be provided to students with a range of abilities within the same block of time. For example, within the same class, one student may be working in Lexia: Strategies for Older Students (Lexia SOS) to practice basic decoding skills, while another student might be working to improve fluency using Read Naturally software, and yet another student might be reading Start to Finish Books to practice comprehension strategies they have been taught in their language arts class. Regardless of the software selected, it is important to remember that CAI does not replace instruction—teachers will need to closely monitor student performance and provide instruction and supports as appropriate (Kennedy & Deshler, 2010; Regan, Berkeley, Hughes, & Kirby, 2013).

Students are expected to read for understanding throughout the school day, even when they are still working toward mastery of basic skills. Teachers need to be cognizant of the basic reading skills of students in their classes and the demands of text that they are expecting students to read and understand. This will enable teachers to purposefully select reading materials and provide accommodations that ensure that all students can gain access to the assigned text.

HOW DO I SELECT TEXTS FOR STUDENTS THAT ARE NOT PROFICIENT IN BASIC READING SKILLS?

Educators often refer to the student's reading level when discussing selection of text. It is important to note, however, that the word *level* can have different meanings depending on the context. A reading level can refer to student proficiency/performance or to the difficulty of the text itself. These types of levels represent different concepts, even though they are referred to interchangeably.

Student Reading Levels

When a student is referred to a reading specialist or a special education teacher for concerns with reading, often an informal reading assessment (i.e., Developmental Reading Assessment, Qualitative Reading Inventory) is

Program	Program description	Grades	Phonemic awareness	Phonics	Fluency	Vocabulary	Comprehension	Spelling	Progress monitoring
Corrective Reading	The Corrective Reading program provides concentrated remedial instruction for elementary or secondary students who experience difficulties in decoding and reading comprehension (http://www.mcgraw-hill.co.uk/sra/correctivereading.htm).	3–12	X	X	X	X	X	X	X
Language!	Language! is an integrative reading intervention designed to support students in 3rd–12th grade who score below the 40th percentile on standardized tests. Language! incorporates intensive support in reading, writing, spelling, vocabulary, grammar, and spoken English (http://www.voyagerlearning.com/curriculum/literacy-solutions/LANGUAGE).	3–12	X	X	X	X	X	X	X
Read 180	Read 180 is designed for students reading two or more years below grade level. This program equips teachers with curriculum, instruction, assessment, and professional development, as well as adaptive technology for differentiation of instruction (http://read180.scholastic.com/reading-intervention-program).	4–12		X	X	X	X	X	X
Rewards	Rewards is a multisyllabic word reading program designed for intermediate and secondary students to teach strategies for decoding complex words and increase oral and silent reading fluency (http://store.cambiumlearning.com/rewards/).	4–12		X	X	X	X		X
Wilson Reading System	The Wilson Reading System is a research-based remedial program for reading and writing. The highly structured, intensive curriculum targets decoding and spelling skills. The system provides direct instruction in teaching total word structure in a multisensory fashion (http://www.wilsonlanguage.com/).	2–12	X	X	X			X	X

Figure 2.1. Common reading programs used in remedial reading classes.

administered to evaluate the student's reading. Most informal reading inventories give an indication of whether a text is at a level that is independent (relatively easy), instructional (challenging but manageable), or frustrational (difficult) for a student (National Reading Panel, 2000). Passages within the inventory correspond to a grade. If a student scores at an independent level on a passage for a particular grade, then this indicates that the text is easy for the student and should be assigned for independent learning tasks such as homework. If a student scores at an instructional level, then this indicates that the text is just right for the student and should be used for instructional purposes. If a student scores at a frustrational level, then this indicates that the text is too difficult for the student, even with instructional support. Frustrational text should be avoided, or accommodations should be provided to ensure that the student is able to gain access to the text.

For example, in a sixth grade class, Jessica may read a fifth-grade text at the independent level whereas Johnny struggles with the same text because it is at his frustrational reading level. A teacher might use this information about their students to adjust instructional groupings and/or selection of text. Some students, especially those with LD, may also show disparate skill performance when reading part of a text. For example, Marcus may be at the instructional level with decoding the words in an eighth-grade passage but at the frustrational level with comprehension of the same passage. This would indicate that this text would be appropriate if the purpose of the lesson was to work on decoding multisyllable words, but it would likely be too difficult if the purpose was to practice a reading comprehension strategy to improve summarization.

Text Reading Levels

Once a teacher has information from the reading assessment, then a book or text section can be chosen to appropriately match the student's level of reading performance. The level of a book or other printed material relates to the text itself. The text is assigned a level based on the difficulty of the text, which is determined through characteristics such as text length and vocabulary. A teacher may choose one level of text for instructional purposes and another level for homework. A comparison chart of the various leveling systems can be useful when choosing text. Three common leveling systems (guided reading, Developmental Reading Assessment, and lexile) are shown in Table 2.1. Sometimes text is not already leveled; however, there are a variety of ways in which a level can be determined as well as ways in which text can be modified to allow for differentiation of students' reading abilities. Examples of free or easily accessible technology are illustrated in Table 2.2.

WHAT ARE CONSIDERATIONS WHEN MODIFYING TEXT OR PROVIDING ACCOMMODATIONS?

Modifications are changes to the text itself, such as shortening the amount of text, reducing the number of vocabulary words, or simplifying sentence

Table 2.1. Comparison chart of leveled reading systems

Grade	Guided reading levels	Developmental Reading Assessment (DRA) levels	Lexile levels
Kindergarten	A, B, C	A-1–4	BR–70
1	D, E, F, G, H, I, J	6–18	80–450
2	J, K, L, M	18–28	451–650
3	N, O, P	30–38	651–770
4	Q, R	40	771–860
5	S, T, U, V, W	40–50	861–980
6	W, X, Y	60	980–1050
7	Z	70	850–1099
8	Z	80	900–1150
9			1000–1199
10			1025–1200+
11			1050–1300+
12			1075–1400+

No specific Developmental Reading Assessment or guided reading levels are assigned above eighth grade.

Table 2.2. Evaluating and making text accessible using free or easily accessible technology

Evaluating and modifying difficulty of text	
Readability Statistics (Microsoft Word)	This tool counts the number of words and paragraphs, averages the number of characters in a word or number of sentences in a paragraph, and calculates readability of text.
AutoSummarize (Microsoft Word)	This tool summarizes key points of reading material. The teacher can determine the length of the summary based on the individual student's reading ability level.
Making text accessible	
Text-to-speech	Text-to-speech functions are available in many word processing programs and provide the capability for text to be read aloud. Reading rate and voice options, as well as background colors and contrast, are often available options.
Viewing and manipulating digital text	Many options within word processing programs and web browsers (e.g., full screen, print layout, outline view, web layout, draft view) are available to customize viewing of digital text to accommodate various reader needs. Fonts, color, text style, and zoom options can also be altered as needed. Installation of free readability add-ons may be required to perform some functions.

Source: Berkeley and Lindstrom (2011).

structures. The text remains intact when accommodations are provided, but students gain access to the text differently, such as using text-to-speech books or audiobooks, highlighting text, or selecting hyperlinks to vocabulary definitions. Although modifying text or making accommodations so that students can gain access to text can be appropriate in some contexts, it is important for teachers to be thoughtful when making decisions about text. Teachers particularly need to consider whether modifying text helps the student meet the objectives of the learning activity. There are two basic questions to ponder: 1) "What is the purpose of this activity?" and 2) "Will text modifications enhance or impede student progress toward the learning objective?" For example, if the purpose of the activity is to understand a complex plot structure in a novel being read by the class, then reducing the amount of text that the student reads may undermine the main learning objective. Instead, it may be more beneficial to allow the student to gain access to the text on tape while reading along with the text.

In contrast, if the main purpose of the instructional activity is to work on reading decoding and fluency, reading a grade-level text is likely to be too difficult for a student that is already reading far below grade level. Reading the text aloud to the student (or providing audio versions of text) will remove this important practice time that the student needs if reading gains are to be made. It may be more appropriate to modify text for this learning objective so that it is at the student's instructional, rather than frustrational, level.

WHAT ARE OTHER CONSIDERATIONS FOR SELECTING TEXTS FOR STRUGGLING READERS?

Interest in the subject of the selected reading material can also be critically important for students with reading problems because engagement in a subject can help a struggling reader persist with reading even when the text is difficult (Jennings et al., 2010). Therefore, teachers should make reading materials available that are interesting and personally meaningful to students. Today there are many collections that are available that target reluctant readers (see Table 2.3). Topics in these collections are of high interest for older students but are written at a lower readability level (Gillet, Temple, & Crawford, 2004). Materials are also emerging that are more representative of students from other cultures.

"Any book that helps a child to form a habit of reading, to make reading one of his deep and continuing needs, is good for him."

Maya Angelou, American author and poet

In addition to selecting reading materials at students' independent reading levels, teachers should consider using high-interest/low-readability materials as part of the primary classroom instruction. Trade books are a staple

Table 2.3. Low-level, mixed-level, and high-interest readers

Series name	Target grade levels	Type of text (narrative, expository, both)	Topics	High interest? (yes, no)	Low level? (yes, no)
24/7 Science Behind the Scenes	8–12	Both	The science and technology used to solve real-life crimes and mysteries	Yes	Yes (Grades 5–7)
Children's Press High Interest Books	7–12	Both	Armed forces, natural disasters, survivors, animals, racing, outdoor life, and top-secret jobs	Yes	Yes (Grades 4–7)
Frank Schaffer High Interest/ Low Readability Workbooks	Middle school	Narrative	Action adventure and biographies	Yes	Yes
Connections Series	Middle and high school	Expository	Designed for use in the content areas	Unclear	Yes (Grades 5–8)
Keystone Books	5–9	Both	Science fiction, sports, horror, suspense, and humor	Yes	Yes (Grades 2–3)
Orca Currents	Middle school (ages 10–14)	Narrative	Middle school fiction	Yes	Yes (Grades 2–4)
Orca Currents	High school	Narrative	Teen fiction	Yes	Yes (Grades 2–4)
HIP Books (Junior)	4–6	Narrative	High action (no real violence)	Yes	Yes (Grades 2–3)
HIP Books (Senior)	7–12	Narrative	High action, teenage problems	Yes	Yes (Grades 3–4)
Remedia Publishing	Elementary through high school	Both (some include audio CDs)	Wide range of topics	Yes	Yes

in elementary school classrooms where teachers have a wide range of texts (called text sets) available within a particular genre (e.g., fables, tall tales). This same idea can be utilized in middle and high school content area classes by creating text sets around topics (e.g., the Civil Rights movement, the water cycle); this is sometimes referred to as *wide reading*. The focus of study becomes concepts rather than the content of a specific textbook (Ivey, 2002). In addition, Tovani (2004, p. 43) noted that text sets

- Contain a wide variety of written texts
- Contain materials that vary in length, difficulty, and text structure
- Contain examples of texts that are relevant, interesting, and accessible to most students

- Give students several options for obtaining information
- Provide opportunities for students to practice reading strategies and learn content information

The availability of a wide range of materials can be beneficial for readers that are not proficient in basic reading skills and can remove this factor as a barrier to comprehension.

Teach Vocabulary

There is an important reciprocal relationship between vocabulary knowledge and comprehension. Vocabulary knowledge plays an important role in lessening comprehension difficulties and, conversely, a lack of vocabulary knowledge can increase problems with comprehension. It is therefore important that teachers directly teach key vocabulary as part of instruction.

WHAT IS VOCABULARY AND WHY IS IT IMPORTANT FOR READING COMPREHENSION?

Vocabulary is the set of words in a language that a person knows and uses. Within the context of reading, these are words that the individual recognizes and knows the meaning of. Vocabulary plays an important role in reading comprehension. The greater the students' vocabulary, the more likely they will comprehend what they read (Klingner et al., 2007; Nagy & Scott, 2000). Conversely, if students do not know the meanings of most of the words they encounter, then they cannot understand what they read (Pullen & Cash, 2011). Children enter school with large differences in vocabulary knowledge, largely due to differences in exposure to vocabulary-rich language (Graves, 2000; Hart & Risley, 1995). These differences continue to increase over time, making the need for direct vocabulary instruction even more pressing for students with language barriers due to learning disabilities (LD) or second language (L2) development (i.e., English language learners, [ELLs]).

Good readers typically develop vocabulary through indirect learning, which includes exposure to new vocabulary through reading. Students with larger vocabularies tend to read more (thus exposing them to more novel vocabulary and concepts), and students who read more tend to have larger vocabularies. However, the inverse is true as well. Students with limited vocabularies tend to read less, and students who read less tend to have more limited vocabularies. Why is this the case? To illustrate, consider the following. If the average fifth grader reads for 25 minutes a day, he or she will read approximately 1 million words. Of those words, if only 1 out of 20 unknown words is learned, that would still total 1,000 new words per year (Anderson & Nagy, 1991). Students who do not frequently read miss the opportunity to be exposed to and learn a tremendous amount of new vocabulary (Baker, Simmons, & Kame'enui, 1998). Stanovich posited that this reciprocal relationship is a version of the Matthew Effect—the idea that the "rich get richer, and the poor get poorer" (1986, p. 382; see Text Box 3.1 for more information on the Mathew Effect.) Therefore, it is important that students expand their vocabulary through direct, explicit instruction of vocabulary (Berkeley & Scruggs, 2010), in addition to indirect learning experiences.

The amount of daily reading significantly decreases when a student reads below grade level. Cunningham and Stanovich (1998) noted that the average fifth grader whose reading is at the

- 30th percentile reads for 1.3 minutes a day (106,000 words per year)

- 10th percentile reads for 0.1 minutes a day (8,000 words per year)

- 2nd percentile does not read at all

This clearly limits the opportunities that poor readers have to learn new vocabulary through reading. Large numbers of these students are those with LD. Students with LD also may not benefit from reading to the same extent as their peers because of deficiencies in skills necessary for proficient and efficient reading, including phonemic awareness, decoding, fluency, and comprehension (Wong, 2004).

A similar effect is seen with students who are ELLs. The majority of ELLs living in the United States come from households where English is not spoken fluently, or not spoken at all, and where parents often do not have the educational levels needed to fully support the learning of academic words; thus, the only exposure these children have to academic words is through school texts. Longitudinal studies have shown that children born in the United States to Spanish immigrants (who were enrolled in U.S. schools since preschool or the primary grades) started out with low vocabulary skills and remained below national norms, with levels not sufficient to reach age-appropriate levels by the time students reached early adolescence. Furthermore, there was a striking discrepancy between ELLs' word reading (on grade) and vocabulary levels (below grade level) by the time they reached early adolescence (Mancilla-Martinez & Lesaux, 2011).

Underdeveloped vocabulary becomes insufficient to support effective reading comprehension and writing and, in turn, has a negative impact on overall academic performance (Lesaux & Marietta, 2012). Thus, given the important role that vocabulary plays in reading comprehension, students must not only receive adequate word reading skills instruction but also instruction that directly promotes vocabulary acquisition.

DIG DEEPER

The Matthew Effect

The Matthew Effect is a phrase that often is referenced in education. It has Biblical origins in the Gospel of Matthew in which it is stated, "For unto every one that hath shall be given, and he shall have abundance; but from him that hath not shall be taken away even that which he hath" (Matthew 25:29). Walberg and Tsai (1983) first coined the phrase the Matthew Effect to describe how some children naturally develop strong foundational achievement skills, which leads to continual academic growth and development, whereas other children who lack early achievement fail to naturally progress.

Early achievements tend to promote a positive trajectory over time, whereas the lack of early success inhibits growth. The Matthew Effect can be true in many aspects of human development, but often is referred to in education subjects such as reading, writing, and math. Keith Stanovich described the Matthew Effect in relation to reading as "the rich get richer, and the poor get poorer" (1986, p. 382).

This graph of the Matthew Effect in reading illustrates the trajectory of reading success in the early elementary grades of those students who enter school with and without foundational reading skills (Wren, 2003). This trend in reading performance continues into the upper grades as well.

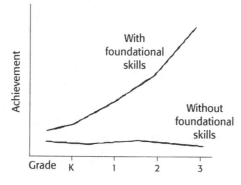

Figure 3.1. Matthew Effects in reading. (From Wren, S. [n.d.] *Developing research-based resources for the balanced reading teacher.* Austin, TX: Author; reprinted by permission.)

Children enter school with a diverse range of abilities in the academic areas of language, literacy, and number skills, as well as social, motor, emotional, and self-regulatory development (Baumert, Nagy, & Lehmann, 2012). Hindman, Erhart, and Wasik (2012) explained that children who live in poverty are especially vulnerable to the Matthew Effect. These children often enter kindergarten lacking foundational literacy and language skills. They may be at a disadvantage in these areas due to limited availability of word-learning opportunities and literacy materials, exposure to traditional and environmental print, and early learning environments (Hindman et al., 2012). Inequalities among students have a tendency to be cumulative in nature over time. These students will continue to lag behind their middle-income peers, with higher probabilities of grade retention, school failure, and special education referrals, without effective early intervention and quality reading experiences.

From Wren, S. (n.d.) *Developing research-based resources for the balanced reading teacher.* Austin, TX: Author; adapted by permission.

WHAT TYPES OF VOCABULARY
WORDS SHOULD BE EXPLICITLY TAUGHT?

It is not feasible to provide direct explicit instruction of every word that a student needs to know. Instead, the National Reading Panel (2000) recommended that teachers focus on three types of words:

1. Important words (e.g., specific academic vocabulary)

2. Useful words (e.g., high-frequency words)

3. Difficult words (e.g., multiple meaning, idiomatic expressions)

Important words can consist of both academic terms and "big idea" words (Feldman & Kinsella, 2005). Programs of study for a curriculum provide guidance for teachers about terminology that students are expected to learn at a particular grade level. This includes content-specific vocabulary terms that are particular to a specific academic area (e.g., science-, math-, or history-specific words such as photosynthesis, parallelogram, or legislature). In addition, big idea words that are essential for student understanding of text are also important, and as such, teachers should preview assigned text to identify academic and content-specific words that students will need to know in order to comprehend the text (Denton, Vaughn, Wexler, Bryan, & Reed, 2012).

Useful words include both high-frequency words and general academic words. As it sounds, *high-frequency words* are those words that appear frequently in text. In fact, 100 high-frequency words (e.g., they, and, before, where, because) make up more than 50% of the words in average texts. Useful words also include general academic words. These words frequently occur in academic texts but may not be specific to one particular content area (e.g., identify, principle, passage).

Difficult words include words that have multiple meanings and idiomatic expressions. For example, the word *scale* can have multiple meanings. It can refer to a scale of a fish (or the action of removing scales from that fish), an instrument used to weigh things, the legend indicating ratio of distance on a map, or even the rate of monetary compensation (a pay scale). Idiomatic expressions are common sayings within a language that cannot be determined by the words themselves—cultural context is needed. For example, the expression "hard to swallow" has nothing to do with the act of swallowing; rather, it is an indication that something is difficult to believe. The expression "raining cats and dogs" refers to a downpour, and "hold your horses" means slow down. Multiple meaning words and idiomatic expressions can be particularly challenging for students with language processing challenges and students who are learning English as a second language, who have limited lexicons (Denton et al., 2012; Snow & Kim, 2007).

WHAT INSTRUCTIONAL TECHNIQUES CAN
HELP STUDENTS LEARN IMPORTANT VOCABULARY?

Strong vocabulary development can be supported through a combination of activities, including 1) wide reading, 2) activities that increase word consciousness—interest in and awareness of words, 3) instruction in how to independently learn words when reading, and 4) direct instruction in content-specific (i.e., important words) and high-utility words—words that appear across the curriculum (Graves, 2006; Torgesen et al., 2007). Although wide reading is important for the reasons previously noted, all students do not read proficiently, and as a result, these students tend to read less. Therefore, it is especially important that teachers select appropriate texts and help students learn how to select appropriate texts for themselves (see Chapter 2 for suggestions in how to select and modify text for students who are not yet reading on grade level). Examples of activities and instructional methods used to promote vocabulary development are presented next.

"The most important thing is to read as much as you can, like I did. It will give you an understanding of what makes good writing and it will enlarge your vocabulary."

J.K. Rowling, author of the Harry Potter series

Word Walls

A word wall is a classroom display of words that have been introduced to students. Word walls serve as a visual reminder to students to incorporate new vocabulary into their reading, writing, and speech (Dougherty Stahl, & Stahl, 2012). Word walls are often liked by students because they typically are built together by the teacher and the students and students have a say on what words should be posted. Although word walls are commonly found in primary classrooms (see Figure 3.2), they also are a useful practice in the upper grades for supporting learning of both content-specific and general academic vocabulary.

Word walls in the upper grades do not need to be alphabetically organized as they are in the primary grades; instead, they may be organized by concepts or units. Figure 3.3 is an example of a word wall in a seventh-grade health class of various types of systems (e.g., circulatory system, digestive system). Some teachers choose to update these word walls at the beginning of a unit, whereas others introduce new words on a specific day of the week, and still others add new vocabulary to the word walls as they come up in instruction. However the teacher chooses to add words, the word wall should be a tool frequently referred to by both teacher and students (Beck, McKeown, & Kucan, 2013).

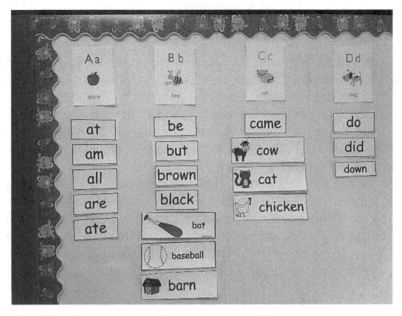

Figure 3.2. Example of a word wall in an elementary school classroom.

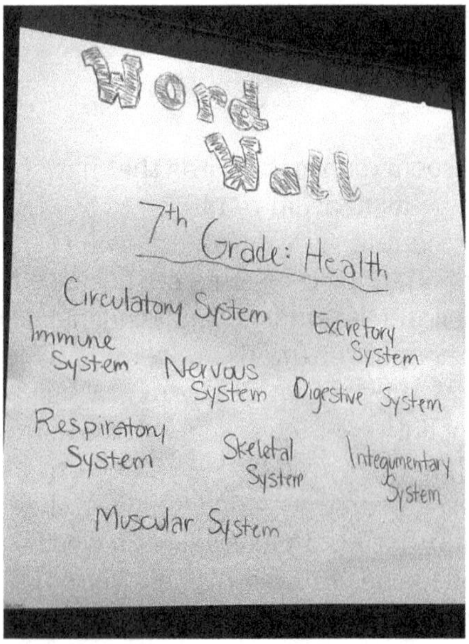

Figure 3.3. Example of a word wall in a seventh-grade health classroom.

Morphemic Analysis

Knowledge of affixes and familiarity with Greek and Latin roots can help students understand the meaning of new words (McEwan, 2008). To illustrate, let's review the nature of words. A *morpheme* is the smallest unit of a word that has meaning. Words can be made up of free morphemes (e.g., the word *cat*) and bound morphemes (e.g., the *-s* in *cats,* which changes the meaning of the word to more than one cat). Free morphemes are often referred to as the *root word* (or *base word*). Bound morphemes generally are referred to as *affixes* (prefixes at the beginning of words and suffixes at the ending of words); they are called bound morphemes because these word parts only have meaning when attached (bound) to a root word. There are numerous prefixes commonly found in English, such as

- *dia-* means *across* or *through* (e.g., diaphragm, diagram)
- *mis-* means *wrong* or *bad* (e.g, mistake, miscount)
- *oct-* means *eight* (e.g., octagon, octopus)
- *pre-* means *before* (e.g., preset, preamble)
- *re-* means *again* (e.g., remake, restart)
- *sub-* means *under* (e.g, submarine, subatomic)
- *un-* means *not* (e.g, unwanted, unnecessary)

Common suffixes in English include

- *-dom* means *quality of* (e.g., freedom, wisdom)
- *-ist* means *someone who does* (e.g., chemist, dentist)
- *-ive* means *being able to* or *having* (e.g., reactive, positive)
- *-ment* means *result* or *product* (e.g, agreement, improvement)
- *-ness* means *quality of* (e.g., hardness, darkness)
- *-s, -es* means *plural* (e.g., planets, batches)
- *-tion* means *act* or *the state of* (e.g., motion, location)

Prefixes generally change the meaning of the root word or make it more specific, whereas suffixes change the number, affect verb tense, indicate comparison, denote possession, or change the grammatical category (Fox, 2010). Identifying and segmenting multisyllable words into these parts is referred to as *structural analysis,* and identifying and determining meanings of words based on the meanings of the parts is referred to as *morphemic analysis* or *word analysis.*

Why should teachers target roots based on Latin and Greek? Modern English (as well as Spanish, French, Italian, and the other Romance languages) is grounded in Latin and Greek, which is why

- Most of the academic words in English (e.g., math and science words) are derived from Latin and Greek.
- Most of the more challenging multisyllabic words in English are derived from Latin and Greek.
- A single Latin or Greek root or affix (word pattern) can be found in, and aid in the understanding of, 20 or more English words (in addition to aiding with decoding and encoding).
- Because Spanish is also a Latin-based language, Latin (and Greek) can be used as a bridge to help Spanish-speaking students use knowledge of their native language to learn English. (Rasinski, Padak, Newton, & Newton, 2011, p. 134)

Latin and Greek roots are commonly found in English. Examples of Latin roots include

- *-aqua-* means *water* (e.g., aquifer, aquatic)

- *-circum-* means *around* (e.g, circumference, circumnavigate)

- *-fract-* means *to break* (e.g., fracture, fraction)

- *-mit-* means *to send* (e.g, submit, remit)

- *-scribe-* means *to write* (e.g., inscribe, transcribe)

- *-struct-* means *to build* (e.g, construct, instruction)

- *-vis-* means *to see* (e.g., television, visible)

Examples of Greek roots are

- *-auto-* means *self* (e.g., autograph, automated)

- *-bio-* means *life* (e.g., biology, biographer)

- *-homo-* means *same* (e.g., homophone, homogenous)

- *-hydr-* means *water* (e.g., hydrogen, dehydration)

- *-logy* means *study* of (e.g, mythology, psychology)

- *-micro-* means *small* (e.g., microscopic, microphone)

- *-therm-* means *heat* (e.g., thermostat, thermos)

Vocabulary Logs

Vocabulary logs (sometimes called vocabulary notebooks) are a useful tool for supporting students' vocabulary development (Bear, Invernizzi, Templeton, & Johnston, 2000; Beck et al., 2013; Marzano, Norford, Paynter, Pickering,

≡ Vocabulary Log

Name Melisa   Period 3

Book Title The Giver   Date 5/21/13

Word (page number & location)	Write out the sentence in which the word appears	What you think the word means	Dictionary definition
palpable p.3 2nd paragraph	Now, thinking about the feeling of fear as he pedalled home along the river path, he remembered that moment of palpable, stomach-sinking terror when the aircraft had streaked above.	something that can make you feel horrible	so intense as to be almost touched or felt
hatchery p.4 top	I left home at the correct time but when I was riding along near the hatchery, the crew was separating some salmon.	a place where salmon live	a place where the hatching of fish or poultry eggs is artificially controlled for commercial purposes
tunic p.4 top	He smoothed his rumbled tunic and sat down.	shirt	a loose garment, typically sleeveless & reaching to the wearer's knees, as worn in ancient Greece & Rome
usages p.6 middle	They were learning usages that my group hadn't learned yet, so we felt stupid.	things you use	habitual or customary practice, esp. as creating a right, obligation or standard

Figure 3.4. Example of a vocabulary log from a middle school English class.

& Gaddy, 2001). When using vocabulary logs as part of instruction, teachers encourage students to

- Find unknown words in their reading, whether that be textbooks, novels, or other sources of information

- Mark unknown words with a question mark and come back to them after finishing reading the text

- Record the word and the sentence from text in the vocabulary log

Students might also record a dictionary definition, their own description of the word, and/or a nonlinguistic representation (picture) that is associated with the word. Figure 3.4 is an example of a vocabulary log from a middle school English class.

Semantic Organizers

There are many forms of semantic organizers (also referred to as *semantic maps*) that a teacher could use to reinforce vocabulary development. One of the most valuable aspects of using these graphic organizers for vocabulary instruction is the conversation that emerges about the words which in turn results in a deeper understanding of the meaning of the word (Fountas & Pinnell, 2001). There are a variety of possible semantic organizers to help students more deeply understand new vocabulary words, including word webs, hierarchical maps that show the target word's relationship to other words, and tables with two columns labeled "is" and "is not" in which the students identify synonyms and antonyms of the target word. The Frayer Model is one commonly used semantic organizer that is comprised of four parts—definition, characteristics, examples, and nonexamples. Figure 3.5 shows examples of this type of semantic organizer used to teach and reinforce math and science vocabulary.

Irrespective of which semantic organizer the teacher chooses to use, the following four steps are generally used in a semantic mapping lesson:

1. The teacher and students brainstorm words and ideas that relate to the target word, and these ideas are recorded on the board.

2. These new ideas are categorized and reorganized into a map.

3. After creating the map, the class reads about the target word.

4. Existing categories are revised or reorganized to incorporate new ideas generated by the reading (Dougherty et al., 2012).

Semantic Feature Analysis

A graphic organizer is also used in semantic feature analysis. Semantic feature analysis has been demonstrated to be effective with diverse groups of students (Baumann, Kame'enui, & Ash, 2003). This strategy

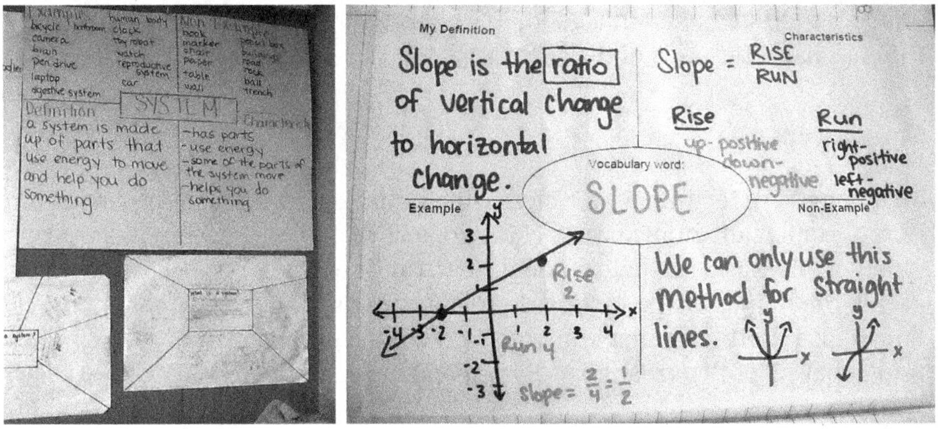

Figure 3.5. Example of a Frayer Model for target words *system* and *slope*.

involves using a chart or grid to categorize words according to aspects of the words' meaning(s). It is intended to help students recognize relationships among key concepts. Students gain a deeper understanding of the targeted vocabulary words by comparing and contrasting words related to a major concept.

Terms are listed across the top and characteristics down the left-hand side (or vice versa) of the chart. Each term and characteristic is discussed, and teachers and students indicate whether there is a positive relationship (noted with a +), a negative relationship (noted with a -), or both (noted with a +/-). Teachers can also use this as a prereading activity and use a question mark to indicate when relationships are unclear. After reading, students can go back and amend the chart. The discussions that result from the activity are important for student learning. Figure 3.6 shows how semantic feature

	Equilateral Triangle	Isosceles Triangle	Scalene Triangle	Right Triangle	Acute Triangle	Obtuse Triangle
3 sides	+	+	+	+	+	+
3 angles add up to 180°	+	+	+	+	+	+
All sides equal	+	-	-	-	+/-	+/-
All angles equal	+	-	-	-	+/-	-
Has a right (90°) angle	-	+/-	+/-	+	-	-
All angles < 90°	+	+/-	+/-	-	+	-

Figure 3.6. Semantic feature analysis for characteristics of different triangles. (From Berkeley, S., & Scruggs, T.E. [2010]. Current practice alerts: A focus on vocabulary instruction. *Division for Learning Disabilities [DLD] and Division for Research [DR] of the Council for Exceptional Children, Issue 18*; reprinted by permission.)

analysis might be used in a geometry class to help students understand the salient characteristics of different types of triangles.

Mnemonics

Mnemonics are techniques for increasing initial learning and long-term retention of important information (Mastropieri & Scruggs, 1991). A variety of mnemonic devices can help students learn and remember important concepts and vocabulary. For example, a fourth-grade teacher might teach students how to use a letter strategy mnemonic during a geography unit to help them remember all of the great lakes by remembering the word HOMES:

Huron

Ontario

Michigan

Erie

Superior

A pictorial representation often is used to further help students remember the letters in the mnemonic. For example, a seventh-grade science teacher might show students a picture of a "penny man" when teaching them a letter strategy for remembering the six types of energy using the mnemonic Mr. Cent (see Figure 3.7):

Mechanical

Radiant

Chemical

Electric

Nuclear

Thermal

Mr. Cent

Figure 3.7.   Mnemonic Mr. Cent for types of energy.

The acrostic is another type of mnemonic. In this type of mnemonic, a sentence is created in which the first letter of each word represents the first letter in the target word. For example, Algebra teachers often teach students the sentence "Please, excuse my dear Aunt Sally" to help them remember the correct order of operations. The first letter in each word of the sentence represents the operations in the correct order:

Please, excuse my dear Aunt Sally

Parentheses, exponents, multiplication, division, addition, subtraction

Mnemonic devices can also be used to help students learn and remember important vocabulary and concepts. The key word method is a mnemonic device that has been well documented within the literature as being effective for vocabulary acquisition, particularly for students with LD (Bryant, Goodwin, Bryant, & Higgins, 2003; Jitendra et al., 2004). This device works by making unfamiliar words or concepts more familiar by strengthening the encoding and retrieval of information. Figure 3.8 is an example of a mnemonic that might be used in a high school French class.

The following steps are followed when creating a mnemonic device:

1. Reconstruct the target word into a key word that is 1) acoustically similar, 2) already familiar, 3) easily pictured, and 4) concrete. The target word *la pomme* in Figure 3.8 sounds like pom pom, which was selected as the key word. Pom poms are used by cheerleaders at many sporting events and are familiar to most students. Furthermore, pom poms are concrete and easily pictured.

2. Relate the key word to the target word in an interactive picture, image, or sentence. The key word (pom pom) is pictured with the target word (apple).

3. Retrieve the appropriate response by thinking of the key word, the picture, and what was happening in the picture to enable recall of the target word. A student would be taught the following steps to retrieve the definition. "What does *la pomme* mean? La pomme sounds like pom pom, so I will think of the picture of the pom poms. What else was in the picture with the pom poms? An *apple*! So la pomme means apple."

Reviews of research consistently have shown that key word mnemonics is an effective practice for teaching vocabulary (e.g., Brigham & Brigham, 2001; Bryant et al., 2003; Jitendra et al., 2004).

apple   **la pomme
(pom pom)**

Figure 3.8. Key word mnemonic used in a foreign language class
La pomme (sounds like pom pom) means *apple* in French.

WHAT ARE POTENTIAL PROBLEMS WITH STUDENTS' UNDERSTANDING OF VOCABULARY?

Low levels of vocabulary knowledge have often been identified as a key barrier to successful comprehension among struggling readers, including ELLs and students with LD (Garcia, 1991; Nagy, 1997; Roth, Speece, & Cooper, 2002; Stahl & Nagy, 2006). Therefore, explicitly teaching vocabulary as part of the reading process is widely recommended as an instructional best practice. There are cautions, however, that teachers should be aware of when teaching vocabulary.

 Caution 1

Be aware that there are limitations in the research base. Although some vocabulary interventions are well established in the research literature (e.g., mnemonics), other interventions currently have a limited research base with some populations. For example, although morphemic analysis generally is considered a promising practice, the research on this practice with students with LD has had mixed findings (Ebbers & Denton, 2008). LD researchers (e.g., Vaughn et al., 2000) stressed the importance of controlling task difficulty for this intervention—such as beginning with easier skills such as inflectional suffixes (-*s, -ed*) and common prefixes (*pre-, dis-, semi-*) before introducing more complex derivational suffixes (suffixes that change the word base, such as when *song* becomes *sing* or *electric* becomes *electricity*). Because students with learning challenges tend to be rigid in thinking, using examples and nonexamples can be effective for helping students effectively apply what they have learned. Positive examples of *tri-* as a prefix that means *three* could be *tricycle, triangle,* and *triplets* (even though pronounced differently). Nonexamples would include words such as *tries, trial,* and *tricky.*

Conversely, instruction for ELLs that focuses on root words that are common to their first language (L1) may be particularly beneficial. Teachers can also make specific reference to common cognates as well. Cognates are words that share a similar spelling, pronunciation, and meaning in more than one language (Colorin Colorado, 2007). There are a large number of cognates in Spanish and English—as many as 30%–40% of words. Examples of cognates are *artist* and *artista, dollar* and *dólar,* and *photo* and *foto.* Teachers can use these language similarities to help ELLs from Spanish-speaking households independently recognize words with similar meanings to their L1.

Regardless of the vocabulary instruction technique selected, Beck and colleagues (2013) cautioned against teachers introducing a new vocabulary word by asking students what they think the word means. If students offer a variety of incorrect answers, then these incorrect meanings may stick in the children's minds. Regardless of the specific intervention, the research consistently indicates that systematic and explicit instruction is crucial when working with students with learning challenges. This includes modeling, guided practice, independent practice, and specific explicit feedback (Jitendra et al., 2004; Swanson & Hoskyn, 2001).

⚠ Caution 2

Be careful not to assume students have knowledge or a deeper knowledge of words than they really do. There is large variability in the exposure that students have outside of school to vocabulary-rich language, and the amount of vocabulary that students acquire through reading is strongly related to the amount of reading that students do—either because of motivation or ability. As a result, the vocabulary development of struggling readers can be 10,000 words or more behind their typically developing peers (Stahl & Nagy, 2006).

Furthermore, knowledge of a word is rarely black and white. Most researchers describe vocabulary knowledge as on a continuum (Phythian-Sence & Wagner, 2007), therefore, teachers also need to be careful not to make assumptions that students have a deeper understanding of a word than they really do. Although continuums of vocabulary knowledge are often described or categorized differently (e.g., Beck, McKeown, & Omanson, 1987; Dale, 1965), generally they range from one end of a continuum where a student may have no knowledge of the word whatsoever, to the other end of a continuum where a student may have a deep understanding of the word, including being able to identify the word's meaning out of context, its relationship to other words, and metaphorical uses of the word (Berkeley & Scruggs, 2010). Between these two ends of a continuum, students may display levels of partial understanding, such as having heard a word but not knowing what it means; a general sense of whether a word has a positive or negative connotation; having a narrow perception of a word when it is in context; or being able to recognize the meaning of a word, but not knowing the word well enough to be able to use the word in appropriate situations. It is important for teachers to remember that students do not need the same level of knowledge for every word.

There are additional considerations for vocabulary development for students who are learning a new language. Text Box 3.2 describes a current hypothesis related to language acquisition for ELLs.

What Might This Look Like in the Classroom?

Some teachers focus on vocabulary but face problems when working with students with LD or who are ELLs. Consider the following scenario. End-of-year testing is nearing, so Mrs. King has prepared a series of lessons to review important language arts concepts taught during the school year. She knows that this will be important for helping the students in her eighth-grade basic skills class to do well because all of her students have disabilities that affect learning. In the first lesson, Mrs. King plans to review basic concepts related

Text Box

3.2

DIG DEEPER

Language Acquisition: Application of Krashen's Five Hypotheses

Linguists have developed various theories of second language acquisition (Larsen-Freeman & Long, 1991). Among these theories, the influential concepts and hypotheses of Stephen Krashen have gained popularity because of their intuitive value for teachers in understanding how English language learners (ELLs) acquire a second language. Although many of Krashen's hypotheses have been questioned due to a lack of empirical evidence to support them (see TESOL Quarterly issues 1986–1993 for an extensive review), some have been embraced by ELL teachers and researchers. Krashen (1982) emphasized that language acquisition theory needs to interact with applied linguistic research and the ideas and intuitions of teachers to inform teaching practice. A description of each of these theories with examples of how each are critical for the development of the second language development of ELLs is presented next.

THE ACQUISITION HYPOTHESIS

Learning a language is described as a process that is conscious because it encompasses both the learning of rules and grammatical structures of a language and the ability to talk about them. This is distinct from language acquisition which is viewed as a subconscious process of learning a language with minimal or no awareness of the process (e.g., young children who have no awareness of grammar rules while using the language, rather they have a feel for correct or incorrect statements).

In the classroom, ELLs need to be exposed to a language-rich environment in which students can hear appropriate use of English grammar as well as have visual images (e.g., books, posters, Internet images) for more complex and abstract words. Most important, ELLs should be provided with plenty of opportunities for communication and purposeful interactions with classmates and teachers (e.g., meaningful scenarios, small- and large-group discussions, prompts to initiate conversations, audio-visual materials). ELLs need to receive instruction on the formal elements of oral and written English (e.g., sentence structure, sound–letter correspondences, pronunciation). In addition, teacher corrections of students' errors through explicit modeling or repetition of the student utterance using the correct form or pronunciation is important for second language development.

THE INPUT HYPOTHESIS

The input hypothesis assumes that learners make progress in language development when they are provided with comprehensible input, which consists of an understandable message that has a grammatical structure that is slightly more advanced than their current level of understanding. When implementing this hypothesis, it is sometimes better not to overcorrect ELLs' grammatical errors because some of these are developmental and will be corrected once students have had sufficient practice with the language. For example, many students who are beginning to use English will tend to regularize irregular verbs (e.g., "I breaked the bike") or omit the use of the auxiliary verb (e.g., "I not came to school yesterday"). It is advisable, however, to rephrase their statements by using the correct form.

THE MONITOR HYPOTHESIS

The monitor hypothesis assumes that a learner can monitor and self-correct his or her errors during communication. Three conditions are needed for this to occur

1. The learner must have knowledge of grammatical rules and forms.

2. The learner must focus on correct form.

3. The speaker must have some wait time to focus on form.

In the classroom, students need exposure to correct grammar forms (e.g., rich literature, oral language models) and teachers need to provide the time for students to self-correct in order for students to reflect on grammar and become metacognitive about their language. For example, in the sentence, "All children played outside for hours," a third-grade ELL may misread the verb during a read-aloud by stating, "All child play outside 4 hours." He or she may be able to self-correct due to awareness of the mismatch between the determiner *all* and the noun *child* if given the time to silently reread the sentence.

THE NATURAL ORDER HYPOTHESIS

The natural order hypothesis states that there is a predictable order for the acquisition of certain basic language forms. Teachers should be aware that certain structures of a language are easier to acquire than others, and, therefore, they should present these in a content-rich environment in which the focus is on meaning rather than rote memorization of language rules.

---

to narrative text structures, such as plot, theme, character, setting, and rising and falling action. She reads the first paragraph in the directions aloud for the activity (Segretto, 2002, p. 12):

> The **main idea** of a reading selection is what the passage is mostly about. The author often states the main idea in the first or last few sentences of the first paragraph. However, the author may state the main idea anywhere in the passage. Sometimes the author only suggests the main idea by leaving clues within the passage.

Maria's hand shoots up. "What does *passage* mean?"

Mrs. King is surprised that this word would throw Maria. Mrs. King thinks, *"Passage is a word on virtually every standardized test that students take. Surely she should have figured this word out from the context. She must just need to have her memory jogged."*

"Who can help Maria by explaining what a *passage* is?" Mrs. King queries.

Not one hand goes up.

"Uh oh," Mrs. King thinks. *"Looks like I need to rethink my review lessons!"*

HOW CAN TEACHERS ASSESS STUDENTS' UNDERSTANDING OF VOCABULARY?

In the previous scenario a student self-reported her unfamiliarity with a term, but this does not always occur. Informal vocabulary assessments can be helpful tools for assisting teachers to gauge students' level of vocabulary knowledge about a particular topic. This does not necessarily mean using a formal test, but can be simple and informal checks of students' level of understanding of various words. This could include asking students to sort words into columns: 1) Do not know at all, 2) Have seen or heard—do not know meaning, 3) I think I know the meaning, or 4) I know the meaning (Allen, 1999). This activity can also be modified as a quick warm-up activity so the teacher can quickly assess the entire class at one time. The teacher can present a new word and ask students to give a "thumbs up" if they know the word and could give a definition, a "thumbs sideways" if they have heard the word but are not positive what it means, or a "thumbs down" if they have never heard the word before. These types of assessments generally are most revealing when they contain a variety of words (useful and difficult words in addition to academic vocabulary) and a variety of difficulty levels (words for which students should feel confident about their knowledge of the meaning, words that need to be reviewed, and new content words that may not have been explicitly taught yet).

It is important for teachers to remember the following, regardless of how they choose to gather information about student knowledge:

- Be purposeful in word selection (in addition to important words, this could include useful words and difficult words).

- Know the reader's existing vocabulary knowledge (and/or depth of knowledge).

- Design appropriate instruction that considers both the nature of the words selected for instruction and the existing knowledge of students.

WHAT ELSE DO TEACHERS NEED TO KNOW ABOUT VOCABULARY?

Research has shown that students, especially students with LD and ELLs, are more likely to retain new vocabulary if they have multiple encounters with words, both in similar contexts (e.g., same subject) and across subjects, in ways that are meaningful and contextualized, rather than through memorization exercises (McKeown, Beck, Omanson, & Pople, 1985; Stahl, 1999). Some estimates suggest that students must encounter a word about 12 times to develop a deep understanding of its meaning (McKeown et al., 1985). Programs are beginning to emerge that explicitly target vocabulary instruction across the curriculum. Text Box 3.3 describes one of these programs.

Text Box 3.3

DIG DEEPER

Project Word Generation

Word Generation (http://wg.serpmedia.org/) is a research-based vocabulary program for middle school students that is designed to teach academic words across content areas (e.g., math, science, language arts, social studies). Academic words comprise those words that students encounter in textbooks or academic materials, but do not use or hear in most everyday spoken language (e.g., hypothesize, derive, conclude, deny, infer). In Word Generation two main categories are taught to students on a weekly basis—words that refer to thinking and communicating (e.g., infer, deny) and words that are shared across subjects but have different meanings depending on the content domain (e.g., element, variable). This program has been successful teaching academic vocabulary to middle schoolers because it focuses on only five target words per week and ensures that students have sufficient exposure to the words across reading and speaking activities, highlighting real uses of the words for specific subject matter. In addition, words are introduced in context, via paragraphs that are of interest to young adolescents and are of relevance in the popular media. Capitalizing on developmental gaps that all students, particularly English language learners, have is another reason that projects such as Word Generation succeed in teaching academic vocabulary.

4

Teach to Activate Students' Prior Knowledge and Help Them Make Connections

Students understand and remember more of what they read when they make connections to their previous experiences and existing knowledge (of themselves, other texts, and the world in general). Teachers can help students comprehend text by helping them activate their existing prior knowledge and create common experiences and knowledge during pre-reading activities.

WHAT IS PRIOR KNOWLEDGE AND WHY IS IT IMPORTANT FOR READING COMPREHENSION?

Prior knowledge is a widely used term that refers to "the knowledge, skills, or ability that the students bring to the learning process" (Jonassen & Grabowski, 1993, p. 417). Prior knowledge is often referred to by other terms, including *background knowledge, schema, personal or experiential knowledge, knowledge base,* and *archival memory* (Dochy, Segers, & Buehl, 1999). These terms all relate to the same concept and generally are used interchangeably. The term *prior knowledge* will be used for the purpose of this chapter.

Good readers use their prior knowledge to help them understand what they are reading (Oczkus, 2004). Using prior knowledge is important for reading comprehension because research has demonstrated consistently that students who lack a relevant knowledge base do not comprehend text as well as students who do (Deshler, Ellis, & Lenz, 1996; Goldman & Rakestraw, 2000). Helping students activate prior knowledge is recommended generally as a way to help students make connections between what they already know and what they read. (See Text Box 4.1 for a description of the Schema Theory which explains the relationship between prior knowledge and comprehension). These connections are categorized often as Connections to Self

(Text-to-Self), Connections to Other Texts (Text-to-Text), and Connections to the World (Text-to-World) (Keene & Zimmerman, 2007). Connections to Self relate to the personal knowledge and experiences that a reader brings to the text. Connections to Other Texts refers to connections that students

---

Text Box

DIG DEEPER

Schema Theory and Reading Comprehension

Schema theory is one of the foundational theories that researchers have used to help explain the reading comprehension process. The word *schema* describes how people organize everyday experiences into meaningful patterns by organizing interrelated ideas or concepts (Alverman, Phelps, & Gillis, 2010). For example, your schema for *airports* might include key characteristics of airports (large spaces where people come and go for air travel with ticketing areas and runways), types of airports (international/regional, large/small, modern/old fashioned), and perhaps airports that have some atypical or memorable characteristics (runway built on land over a river). The first researchers of schema theory indicated that knowledge tends to be represented in nested categories so that a schema is often linked to other schemata (plural form), rather than isolated facts (Rumelhart, 1984). One important reason for this organization of your schema for an airport is that it is clustered around big, identifiable ideas (Fisher & Frey, 2009; Rumelhart, 1994). Thus, when you read about a story taking place in an airport, you can easily retrieve your integrated and organized knowledge of airports—your airport schema—which helps you understand the story.

In contrast, consider a topic that is unorganized in your mind (e.g., knowledge of the bamboo plant). You may know a few facts about the bamboo plant, such as it grows in some areas of East Asia, it can be big, and it is one of the favorite foods of panda bears. This may be enough if the topic of bamboo is irrelevant to what you are learning. But if it is central to the learning objective, then your unorganized knowledge is not likely enough to contribute to improved learning.

Schemata are modified as new information is acquired, allowing people to generalize, form opinions, and understand new experiences (Anderson, 1984). Schema is theorized to operate similarly in reading. A person's schema for a topic helps him or her to predict, infer, and evaluate the importance of information, and build relationships between ideas (Alverman et al., 2010). Conversely, missing or incomplete schema can result in problems with reading comprehension. Existing schema that is inconsistent with information that is read can also be problematic. A reader often will ignore ideas that conflict with the reader's prior knowledge, even if this knowledge is inaccurate (Guzzetti & Hynd, 1998). Although more contemporary theories have emerged (e.g., constructivist learning theory, social constructivist learning theory), schema theory continues to influence our understanding of the process of reading comprehension.

make between the text being read and other texts (including knowledge of genre and text structure). Connections to the World includes factual knowledge and experiences that the individual brings to the reading task. This act of making connections helps readers relate new information to existing knowledge, which can result in improved comprehension (Sampson, Rasinski, & Sampson, 2003).

"All experience is an arch to build upon."

Henry Adams, American Historian

WHAT INSTRUCTIONAL TECHNIQUES CAN HELP STUDENTS ACTIVATE PRIOR KNOWLEDGE?

Several instructional approaches often are used by teachers to help students activate their existing knowledge. This instruction generally involves a teacher-led whole-class or group activity (sometimes in combination with a graphic organizer or writing prompt).

Brainstorming is one example of a teacher-led class activity in which a teacher will list items that students share aloud, and then as a class, this shared knowledge is grouped to determine a categorical label. The KWL chart is a more structured form of this (Ogle, 1986). KWL stands for the column headings on a graphic organizer—Know, Want to know, and Learned (see Figure 4.1). Prior to reading, individual students share aloud what they already know (or think they know) about the topic, and students generate questions as a class related to what they want to know after reading the text. Finally after reading, students share what they have learned, and the teacher records student contributions on the graphic organizer.

Know	Want to know	Learned

Figure 4.1. KWL chart.

A Connections Chart is another example of a structured activity intended to activate students' prior knowledge. When creating a Connections Chart, students are encouraged to make connections between what they read and their existing prior knowledge (i.e., connections to self, other texts, the world). Connections that students make while reading are recorded on sticky notes while they read (often with a sentence starter such as, "This reminds me of . . ."). These notes are then transferred to the corresponding connection category on the class chart. Figure 4.2 shows a Connections Chart from a high school language arts class that is reading the novel *In Cold Blood* by

Name <u>Xavier</u>   Date <u>10/25/2013</u>

Title of story <u>In Cold Blood</u>   Author <u>Truman Capote</u>

Making Connections		
Text-to-Self	**Text-to-Text**	**Text-to-World**
1. The character Dick has an attraction to kids, which reminds me of a teacher who was caught soliciting a minor at my school.	The character Perry reminds me of Voldemort in Harry Potter and how he killed innocent people.	The shooter Perry Smith reminds me of the shootings at the movie premier of Batman. He killed them in cold blood.
2. The two men in the story got caught, which reminds me of someone at school getting caught with stink bombs.	The character Dick reminds me of Malfoy in Harry Potter and how he bullies people.	When the two men in the story get caught it reminded me of Saddam Hussein being caught.
3. In the story, the trial took awhile, like it takes awhile when I'm counting down the days to see my favorite band in concert.		When the characters who killed people were on the run it reminded me of when the DC snipers were on the run before they were caught.

| The student makes connections to something personal that happened in his or her life. | The student makes connections to a story he or she has read in the past. | The student makes connections to events that are happening or have occurred in the world. |

Figure 4.2. Connections Chart.

ANTICIPATION GUIDE

Name Ella
Title *You Wouldn't Want to be an American Pioneer!*

Date March 11
Author Jacqueline Morley

1. Before reading, the teacher creates a mix of true and false statements that are answered in the book. The purpose of these statements is to activate students' background knowledge.

2. Before reading the text, students read the statements and indicate whether they agree or disagree. True/false can also be used.

3. After reading the text, the students evaluate whether they were right in agreeing or disagreeing with the statements. This is an opportunity to challenge misconceptions.

4. After determining whether they were right, students reflect. This can be a reflection on why they were wrong (e.g., "I didn't know what buffalo were.") or the statement itself (e.g., "Cholera sounds gross.").

Statement	Agree/ Disagree	Were you right?	Reflect
1. Pioneers traveled alone across America.	disagree	Yes	I didn't know they would make groups.
2. Spring was the best time of year to make the journey across America.	agree	Yes	Then they can get there before winter.
3. One danger pioneers faced was buffalo stampedes.	disagree	No	I didn't know what buffalo were.
4. Pioneers had no trouble finding food on their journey.	agree	No	I thought they would find lots of food.
5. Many pioneers died from cholera, a deadly fever.	agree	Yes	Cholera sounds gross.
6.			
7.			
8.			
9.			
10.			

Figure 4.3. Anticipation guide for an expository text.

55

Truman Capote. (Additional graphic organizers that can be used to foster reading comprehension are presented in Chapter 5.)

Prior knowledge is also often facilitated by asking students to write about what they know about the topic prior to reading. Writing activities range from open-ended "quick writes" (e.g., "Write about what you know about bees.") to specific prereading questions or anticipation guides about the topic. These activities can help the teacher determine how much factual knowledge students have about the topic of the reading. Figure 4.3 is an example of an anticipation guide for an expository trade book, *You Wouldn't Want to be an American Pioneer!* by Jacqueline Morley, used during social studies in a fourth-grade classroom. Figure 4.4 is a guide used in a middle school creative writing class for the novel, *Love That Dog* by Sharon Creech.

ANTICIPATION GUIDE

Name T B   Date 4/9/13
Title Love That Dog   Author Sharon Creech

Read the following statements and respond with **agree** or **disagree** and explain.

Statement	Agree or disagree	Because
Poetry is for girls.	disagree	Anyone can read or write poetry. Poetry is for everyone not just girls.
I am a good writer.	agree	I can write and I'm good at it, but I don't like to.
I like other people to read what I write.	agree	I like to have other people's input if they like what I wrote or what I should change.
Poetry is hard to write.	agree	I find it difficult to write some poetry. But some poetry is easy to write but the majority of it I have trouble writing.
I like to express my feelings when I write.	agree	I find myself to get wordy when I write and when I'm explaining whatever I'm writing about.
I like my teacher to comment on my writing.	agree	I like to have feedback from my teachers on how I did and what they think I should change or do better.

Figure 4.4. Anticipation guide for a narrative text.

WHAT ARE POTENTIAL PROBLEMS WITH STUDENT ACTIVATION OF PRIOR KNOWLEDGE?

What students understand from text and the decisions they make to help themselves understand text (e.g., using a reading comprehension strategy) are related at least in part to their prior knowledge (Pressley et al., 1994). Therefore, helping students activate their prior knowledge as a part of the reading process is often recommended as an instructional best practice. However, research is beginning to show caveats to this type of instruction (Roberts & Duke, 2010). There are cautions that teachers should be aware of when using this practice.

⚠️ Caution 1

Students with reading problems, including students with learning disabilities (LD), often lack the background knowledge, personal experiences, and vocabulary that aid in comprehending core texts (Jennings et al., 2010). For students who are English language learners' (ELLs), limited background knowledge of academic topics and vocabulary can sometimes be due to differences in cultural background and/or curricular experiences (e.g., events that led to the American Revolution, the role of Martin Luther King Jr. in the Civil Rights movement in the United States). Concepts need to be in the student's experience in order to map together ideas (i.e., schema) with the associated terms/labels so that these concepts become part of an integrated knowledge network. Many students, including those with LD and some ELLs, may have the concepts linked to an idea or topic but may lack the labels (vocabulary) to activate that knowledge. Students who lack general and content-specific vocabulary will be hindered in attempts to build an integrated network of *usable* knowledge rather than a list of disconnected facts (National Research Council, 2000). In addition, a lack of prior knowledge can negatively affect both comprehension and interest in reading (Ganske, 2010). Activities such as the ones previously described will not be helpful to a student who does not have relevant prior knowledge to draw from, or worse, these activities could result in misunderstandings about the purpose of activating prior knowledge for some students.

It should be noted that some ELLs may display limited knowledge in English but possess grade-level literacy or academic skills in their first language (L1). This means that ELLs may lack the words in English for certain concepts (e.g., photosynthesis, evaporation, closed circuits), but may have general or specific knowledge of these processes because they read and learned about these concepts in their L1. Academic language or the language of schooling is the language that is used for school tasks and textbooks as the primary medium for instruction (Schleppegrell, 2004). It presents a challenge for both native and nonnative speakers of English because of its decontextualized nature, complexity, and unfamiliarity to many students. Academic language proficiency has been described as part of a common underlying proficiency across languages, in the sense that once knowledge and abilities are acquired in one language, they can potentially become available in the second one (Lanauze & Snow, 1989; Royer & Carlo, 1991). Many academic skills, especially literacy skills, fall into this category. Once certain notions of oral and written language (e.g., phonemic awareness, sound–letter correspondences, concepts of print) are developed in the L1, they can be used to facilitate reading development in another language. Similarly, previously learned academic concepts in the L1, such as the science concepts previously mentioned, provide a stronger basis for learning the terms/words for these concepts in the second language (L2; Moll & González, 1994). Therefore, one of the first things the teacher needs to determine is if the ELL really has limited knowledge of a given topic or if it is masked by limited English proficiency (Moll, 1989). In addition, when students possess prior knowledge in their L1, it is especially important that they are provided access to culturally relevant materials to assist them in integrating new information and vocabulary with concepts and vocabulary that they already know in their L1 (see Text Box 4.2 for examples).

Text Box

4.2

PRACTICAL APPLICATION

Using Culturally Relevant Materials for Activating Prior Knowledge of English Language Learners

English language learners' (ELLs') use of their first language (L1) can be a great tool for helping them build vocabulary in English when they possess both literary and life experiences that allow them to activate and draw from their background knowledge in their L1. In fact, research shows that using their L1 to develop literacy in their second language (L2) is not counterproductive. On the contrary, skills developed in the L1 support reading and writing in English in many ways (Genesee & Geva, 2006; Genesee & Riches, 2006; Reese, Garnier, Gallimore, & Goldenberg, 2000). It is true, however, that ELLs' language proficiency in their L1 and L2 run along a continuum so that some ELLs have a fully developed L1 across speaking, reading, and writing, whereas others may have strong L1 oral language, but may have not developed literacy skills (Gottlieb, Cranley, & Oliver, 2007).

Culturally relevant materials to support activation of prior knowledge of various topics can be either in the L1 or L2. The purpose for using these materials is to help ELLs link known knowledge to new knowledge. The teacher can assist with selecting these in either English or Spanish (or another language if available/necessary), depending on availability and the students' level of English proficiency (see Chapter 1 for a description of language proficiency levels). Teachers using materials written in English should ensure that these culturally relevant materials are accessed before they start a prior knowledge activation activity. This will help students build and activate some knowledge of the topic as well as become familiar with vocabulary and grammar structures of the English language prior to delving into grade-level text reading

(Taboada & Rutherford, 2011). Teachers using materials written in Spanish (or other L1) can capitalize on the use of cognates (e.g., Latin and Greek roots with the same meaning: *accompany–acompañar; balance–balancear; lagoon–laguna; patience–paciencia*). See http://spanishcognates.org for a comprehensive list of Spanish–English cognates to help students preview specific academic vocabulary. Providing a broader schema or frame of reference for the topic to be read in English is the second purpose of using culturally relevant materials in the L1. This activity will require that ELLs have an intermediate to advanced L1 language proficiency. This can become an effective way to address academic vocabulary in advance and give ELLs an opportunity to focus on key concepts of the topic that can facilitate activation of prior knowledge before reading about them in English.

Some examples of books or book series written in Spanish include:

- *La Llorona, The Weeping Woman* by Joe Hayes is a ghost story that has been passed down for hundreds of years in Spanish speaking cultures. It is a tale of caution about a beautiful woman who marries the most handsome man, but does not have a happy ending.
- *¡Yo!* by Julia Alvarez depicts the life story of Yolanda Garcia, who comes from the Dominican Republic to New York.
- Ciencia Grafica published by Capstone is a set of 12 titles narrated by Max Axiom, a scientist with super powers. Max takes the reader on adventures, whether by shrinking down to the size of an ant or riding a sound wave, to explore topics in science.

Examples of culturally relevant books or book series written in English include:

- *The House on Mango Street* by Sandra Cisneros is a coming-of-age story of Esperanza, a Mexican-American girl growing up in Chicago. She writes about her family, her neighborhood, and her life.
- *¡The Surrender Tree: Poems of Cuba's Struggle for Freedom* by Margarita Engle tells the story of a freed slave named Rosa who heals the wounded during the three wars for Cuba's independence. She hid in mountains and caves and healed not only the Cuban soldiers but also the Spanish soldiers.
- Bridge to Reading Zone series published by Capstone includes 20 titles spanning across a variety of topics (i.e., adventure, biography, history, science, sports) for various cultures.
- Summit Books collections published by Perfection Learning capture different topics and include characters with different cultural backgrounds.

 ## Caution 2

Students with reading problems do not effectively use prior knowledge they possess to aid in comprehension (Pace, Marshall, Horowitz, Lipson, & Lucido, 1989). The goal of activating prior knowledge is to help students make connections that increase understanding, but for many students, this prompting results in numerous tangential or inconsequential connections (Harvey & Goudvis, 2000; Roberts & Duke, 2010). For example, when reading a biography of Jacqueline Kennedy, the student might read that Mrs. Kennedy owned a blue car and think, *"We have a blue car, too."* The student is making a connection between the text and his or her own experiences, but that connection is inconsequential because it is not likely to help the student comprehend the important aspects of Jacqueline Kennedy's life that make her an important historical figure. Furthermore, when struggling to understand difficult text, a student who often makes tangential or inconsequential connections is more likely to focus on prior knowledge related to isolated details. In turn, this can lead him or her to make unwarranted inferences about the meaning of the text. This ineffective use of prior knowledge can inadvertently detract from comprehension rather than enhance it. Thus, it is important to keep in mind the key ideas and knowledge to be acquired from the text. Not all connections are fruitful connections.

⚠️ Caution 3

Many students with reading problems tend to overuse their prior knowledge (Williams, 1993). This may not sound like a bad thing on the surface, but overusing prior knowledge can be problematic when students have misconceptions or inaccuracies in their prior knowledge. Students with reading difficulties may have particular trouble using their prior knowledge to modify misconceptions and are resistant to altering their views even when presented with more accurate evidence to support an alternative viewpoint (Alverman, Phelps, & Gillis, 2010; Dochy et al., 1999). In such cases, students' personal points of view and opinions impede their understanding of new information in text, rather than enhance their comprehension (Jennings et al., 2010; Otero & Kintsch, 1992). For example, a student reading about gravity in a science textbook is likely to encounter the fact that objects fall at the same speed regardless of their weight. However, researchers (Champagne, Gunstone, & Klopfer, 1985) have found that students often have the misconception that heavier objects fall faster than lighter objects, and they persist in this belief even when presented with information to the contrary. This misconception is likely to impede the students' understanding of what is read in the science text.

Although many ELLs may display limited prior knowledge more often than overuse their prior knowledge, teachers must be on the lookout for misconceptions that arise from different cultural experiences in the students' home backgrounds. For example, imagine a seventh-grade student who is literate in his L1, but is a newcomer to the United States. Because the student is likely to have attended school in his home country, the idea of what an American *centrist political tendency* means may be different from what he has experienced or previously been taught in his home country's social studies curriculum. This student may not necessarily have limited prior knowledge on the topic, but his schemata on "being politically centrist" could possibly bring ideas on the concept (i.e., associated with centrist tendencies in his cultural milieu) that do not necessarily relate to the typical American notion of this political tendency. This could result in serious misconceptions that the social studies teacher will need to explicitly address in order to ensure that the student accurately understands information read on the topic.

What Might These Problems Look Like in the Classroom?

Many teachers that work with struggling readers, including students with LD and ELLs, have faced problems when implementing prior knowledge lessons in the classroom. Imagine the following scenario:

"Who has been to a circus before?" the teacher asks.

Not one hand is raised.

"Okay. What do you know *about* the circus?" the teacher asks.

Again, not one hand is raised.

"Has anyone *heard* the word circus before?" the teacher asks.

"I have been to Circus Burger before with my Dad. Does that count?" Max volunteers.

The teacher ponders, *"How do I respond to this?"* as the students look at her expectantly.

Many teachers who have faced this type of situation abandon attempts to help students activate prior knowledge before they begin reading; however, this may not be the most helpful decision for struggling readers who are in need of prereading support. Instead, the pitfalls to activating prior knowledge related to individual experiences (that may be limited, inaccurate, or nonexistent) can be mediated by creating shared experiences and knowledge that the teacher helps students create as part of prereading instruction.

HOW CAN TEACHERS HELP CREATE SHARED PRIOR KNOWLEDGE TO SUPPORT INSTRUCTION?

Shared learning is created when experience and learning happen as an entire class and can later be drawn on as a prior knowledge reference when students read challenging texts. Creating shared prior knowledge can be particularly helpful when initially modeling how to use prior knowledge to help with comprehension and, conversely, how information read in text can help to change and refine a reader's prior knowledge base. The examples that the teacher uses to illustrate gaining access to and making connections to prior knowledge are shared by all students in the class. Creating shared experiences is especially important when this is the only prior knowledge that a student has to tap into.

There are many experiences that teachers can construct as part of instruction that can help build the prior knowledge students will need to help them with comprehension of new or challenging text. The following are five ways to create shared prior knowledge:

1. Read-aloud (e.g., picture books, short informational passages)

2. Visual aids (e.g., photographs, diagrams)

3. Multimedia (e.g., video clips, podcasts)

4. Activities (e.g., hands-on activities, field trips)

5. Preteaching vocabulary (e.g., semantic mapping, word webs)

Once this shared prior knowledge has been created, any number of prior knowledge activation activities (including the ones described at the beginning of this chapter) can be used with more meaningful results for all students. In essence, creating shared prior knowledge goes beyond activating prior knowledge by also including the building of prior knowledge. This is an important distinction because "building background knowledge requires that teachers, the architects of their students' learning, create experiences that cause students to bump into, and reconsider, what they know" (Fisher & Frey, 2009, p.115). See Text Box 4.3 for examples of how picture books can be used to create shared background knowledge.

Text Box 4.3

PRACTICAL APPLICATION

Using Picture Books to Create Shared Background Knowledge

BUILD KNOWLEDGE OF DIFFERENT POINTS OF VIEW IN WRITING

The phrase "it depends on your point of view" is relevant in all aspects of life. When reading, recognizing the storyteller's point of view helps the reader make inferences related to character motivation and bias (among other things). This inferencing helps us understand situations at a deeper level and helps us make decisions about whether we should take things at face value or be skeptical. Understanding perspective is an important, but challenging, skill for students to grasp. Purposefully selected short readings with an accompanying activity that highlights the storyteller's point of view can help build important foundational knowledge of point of view prior to beginning reading of more complex text. Using picture books pares down the content to an essential and manageable amount of text that the teacher can read aloud within a single warm-up or introductory lesson. The teacher can then refer to the shared reading as a common framework during instruction, with confidence that all students have at least that basic prior knowledge.

An example of an activity might be comparing James Marshall's traditional version of *The Three Little Pigs* with John Scieszka's alternate version *The True Story of the Three Little Pigs,* written from the perspective of the Big Bad Wolf.

BUILD COMMON FACTUAL KNOWLEDGE OF THE TOPIC

Simply exposing students to factual knowledge related to what they will be reading about can help them make connections and understand more about what they read on that topic. A wide range of nonfiction picture books that have relatively short informational passages with accompanying illustrations are available and can be helpful for this purpose. One student favorite is *Oh, Yuck! The Encyclopedia of Everything Nasty* by Joy Masoff. In addition to interesting information about kid-friendly topics such as blood, body lint, body odor, and burping (and these are just some of the *B* topics), this book also covers a variety of topics that relate to science curricula, including a variety of animals (bats, naked mole rats, snakes), plants (fungi, "vile" vegetation), insects (ants, grubs, lice, worms), and other organisms (bacteria, parasites, viruses).

ADDRESS MISCONCEPTIONS

We do not always know what misconceptions students have in their prior knowledge; however, in some instances a concept is so important for comprehension that the teacher may elect to be proactive. For example, "What characteristics come to mind when you think of a bully?" Many people, especially children, think of the big kid on the playground that beats up other children or steals their lunch money. Although this may be correct, it is not necessarily complete. Mo Willem's *Don't Let the Pigeon Drive the Bus!* is a good illustration of this. In this incredibly funny picture book, the bus driver exits and tells the reader, "Don't let the pigeon drive the bus!" Then enters the pigeon and the first thing that he asks the reader is if he can drive the bus. He begs, he tries to negotiate, he gets upset and gives the reader dirty looks, he tries to make the reader feel sorry for him, he tries to trick the reader, he bargains, he bribes, he gets angry, and finally he threatens. Of course when the bus driver returns, the pigeon leaves as fast as he can. The pigeon is definitely a bully! Students are exposed to these types of manipulations all the time, but many students do not recognize this as a form of bullying. Failing to recognize these characteristics could seriously impede a student's interpretation of character motive and understanding of events that affect a story's plot. A shared picture book reading and discussion can help to redefine students' misperceptions before they begin reading.

MORE WAYS TO USE PICTURE BOOKS
TO CREATE SHARED PRIOR KNOWLEDGE

- Build knowledge of text structure (e.g., narrative, temporal, cause/effect)
- Build knowledge of difficult literary concepts (e.g., foreshadowing, irony)
- Build knowledge of text supports (e.g., table of contents, maps, graphs)
- Build vocabulary

WHAT ARE OTHER ASPECTS OF A
READER'S PRIOR KNOWLEDGE TO CONSIDER?

Prior knowledge generally refers to both knowledge of concepts and facts and knowledge of processes (e.g., how things work, why things happen). Readers also have additional background knowledge related to metacognition, strategies for completing tasks, and informational structures that is important for reading comprehension (Deshler et al., 1996). Metacognition includes students' knowledge of their own strengths and weakness as readers and awareness of task demands. Knowledge of strategies can include cognitive strategies (e.g., self-questioning, summarizing), self-regulation (actively planning, anticipating, and monitoring learning), task-attack strategies (e.g., how to interpret maps and graphs), and problem-solving strategies (e.g., comprehension fix-up strategies, word-attack strategies). Knowledge of information structures can include knowledge of word structures (e.g., affixes) and organizational structures (e.g., narrative and expository text structures). For ELLs, this includes basic knowledge of the components of the English language as discussed in Chapter 1. Descriptions of these additional knowledge structures and related instructional methods that can assist students with reading comprehension are provided in the following chapters.

5

Teach Students to Ask and Answer Questions

Asking and answering questions (questioning) while reading can help students to actively engage with text in the same ways that good readers naturally do. Research has shown that questioning strategies improve student comprehension. Furthermore, questioning is a technique that can help students process information in deeper and more meaningful ways. In addition, questioning can help students synthesize information more efficiently.

WHAT ARE QUESTIONING STRATEGIES AND WHY ARE THEY IMPORTANT FOR READING COMPREHENSION?

Asking and answering questions (questioning) throughout the reading process can assist readers to actively engage with text, self-regulate reading strategies, and understand more of what they read (Berkeley, King-Sears, Vilbas, & Conklin, 2014). Research consistently has shown that strategies that promote active text-related questioning are highly effective for improving student comprehension (e.g., Edmonds et al., 2009; National Reading Panel, 2000). Information is better understood and remembered when students ask and answer questions about the text (Vaughn & Bos, 2009). Thus, the process of asking and answering questions throughout the reading process helps students to actively engage and interact with the text. Furthermore, students are less likely to abandon text when they have questions about it because they are more motivated to find the answers (Harvey & Goudvis, 2000).

"Who questions much, shall learn much, and retain much."

Francis Bacon, philosopher who promoted the scientific method

---

WHAT ARE TYPES OF QUESTIONS THAT TEACHERS SHOULD ASK AND TEACH STUDENTS TO ANSWER?

All questions are not created equal. Different cognitive skills are needed to answer different types of questions. Therefore, it is important to explicitly teach students strategies to answer questions. This typically is accomplished by helping students understand the nature of the question being asked.

Types of Questions

Questions can be conceptualized and classified in numerous ways. For example, questions can require the reader to process information that is explicit (answers are stated within one sentence), implicit (answers are formulated from information stated within two or more sentences), or scriptal (answers are not found in the text, but held within the reader's prior knowledge or experience) (National Reading Panel, 2000). Most informal reading inventories (e.g., Developmental Reading Assessment, Qualitative Reading Inventory) include explicit (literal) and implicit (inferential) questions. Patterns in a student's incorrect responses to these types of questions can give teachers insight into the types of problems the student may be having when reading text. For example, if a student correctly answered inferential questions, but missed explicit questions, then he or she may be having difficulty with memory storage and retrieval. In contrast, if a student correctly answered explicit questions, but missed implicit questions, then he or she may be having difficulty summarizing, making connections within and outside the text (e.g., using prior knowledge), and/or making inferences. Instruction for these two types of students would look very different because their comprehension difficulties stem from different processes.

What do different types of questions look like? Consider the questions that might be asked in a history class that is reading the Gettysburg Address (see Figure 5.1). A teacher might ask students the following questions after reading:

- *What was happening in the country at the time of the speech?* This could be considered an *explicit* question because the answer can be found in one sentence in text.

- *What does the president think could happen if the north does not win the war?* This could be considered an *implicit* question because the reader needs to get a sense of multiple statements made in the text and combine that with his or her prior knowledge (including information from other texts) to infer that the president thinks the country will not remain intact if the north does not win the war.

- *Who gave this speech?* This could be considered a *scriptal* question because this information is not contained in the speech itself; rather, the student would need prior knowledge that President Abraham Lincoln gave this speech.

Four score and seven years ago our fathers brought forth on this continent, a new nation, conceived in Liberty, and dedicated to the proposition that all men are created equal.

Now we are engaged in a great civil war, testing whether that nation, or any nation so conceived and so dedicated, can long endure. We are met on a great battlefield of that war. We have come to dedicate a portion of that field, as a final resting place for those who here gave their lives that that nation might live. It is altogether fitting and proper that we should do this.

But, in a larger sense, we cannot dedicate—we cannot consecrate—we cannot hallow—this ground. The brave men, living and dead, who struggled here, have consecrated it, far above our poor power to add or detract. The world will little note, nor long remember what we say here, but it can never forget what they did here. It is for us the living, rather, to be dedicated here to the unfinished work which they who fought here have thus far so nobly advanced. It is rather for us to be here dedicated to the great task remaining before us—that from these honored dead we take increased devotion to that cause for which they gave the last full measure of devotion—that we here highly resolve that these dead shall not have died in vain—that this nation, under God, shall have a new birth of freedom—and that government of the people, by the people, for the people, shall not perish from the earth.

Figure 5.1.   The Gettysburg Address.

Questions can also be thought of from other perspectives. For example, questions might be viewed as targeting understanding of main ideas or details. In the previous examples, the question, "What does the president think could happen if the north does not win the war?" could be labeled as a *main idea* question because it is the central premise of the entire speech. "What was happening in the country at the time of the speech?" might be considered a *detail* question because it supports the readers' understanding of the central premise.

Alternatively, questions can be viewed as targeting understanding via a hierarchy of skills, such as Bloom's taxonomy (from most to least complex: creating, evaluating, analyzing, applying, understanding, or remembering). In the previous examples, the question, "What does the president think could happen if the north does not win the war?" could be thought of as a *creating* question because it requires the student to create new meaning from the information provided in text and the student's prior knowledge of the topic. "What was happening in the country at the time of the speech?" might be considered a basic *remembering* question. Additional questions within this framework might include, "Why do you think the president decided to give this speech?" (*evaluating*) and "Why is the Gettysburg Address still relevant today?" (*applying*).

Teachers should be thoughtful and intentional in their questioning, regardless of how they decide to categorize these types of questions. It is also important for teachers to consider the functions that questions serve at different points in the reading process. Questions asked prior to reading may be intended to help students activate their prior knowledge; questions during reading might be intended to prompt students to engage with the text and summarize while they read; and questions after reading may be intended to help students integrate what they already know with new information learned through reading. Certainly some questions lend themselves better to each of these purposes.

Helping Students Answer Questions

Teaching students to recognize the nature of questions can help them think about and determine a correct answer to those questions. One way to do this is to explicitly teach students to recognize the relationships between questions and their answers. An example of this strategy is called QAR (Question Answer Relationships). Students are taught to recognize explicit, implicit, and scriptal information through four types of questions:

1. Right there

2. Think and search

3. Author and you

4. On your own

Right there questions ask students to identify information that was directly stated in text. *Think and search* questions and *author and you* questions ask students to identify information that was implied in text and *on your own* questions ask students for information entirely from the students' own background knowledge (Adler, 2001). Helping students identify the nature of what a question is asking can help them decide the best way to approach answering the question. For example, looking back to the text might be a great strategy for finding an answer to a right there question, but it would not be helpful at all for an on your own question. Figure 5.2 shows examples of each type of question with example modeling that a teacher might provide to illustrate the relationship between the question and the answer.

HOW CAN STUDENTS BE TAUGHT TO ASK THEIR OWN QUESTIONS ABOUT TEXT?

Students should also be taught how to develop their own questions during the reading process. Why is it necessary to teach students to ask their own questions about text? Simply put, asking questions helps students understand more of what they read (e.g., National Reading Panel, 2000; Taboada & Guthrie, 2006). When students ask their own question, they set personal goals for finding answers through reading. A student's self-generated questions help to foster his or her own purposes for reading. Readers are likely to be much

"Around 1700, the Lakota began to move west. They found horses and buffalo on the plains in the West. Both animals became very important to the Lakota. They called the horses 'sacred dogs.' The Lakota soon used horses, instead of dogs, to pull their travois because the horses could pull much larger loads. Horses could travel greater distances, too. Most important, the Lakota learned to ride the horses so that they could travel faster and farther. This gave the Lakota an advantage in their wars with other Indians. The Lakota heaped praise on young warriors who captured horses from other tribes."

Question answer relationships

Right there
Why did the Lakota learn to ride horses?

Teacher: If we look back to the text, we can easily find the answer. This is a right there question.

Think and search
In what ways were horses beneficial to the Lakota?

Teacher: This question is different from a right there question because we had to look in more than one place for the answer. So, this is a think and search question.

Author and you
Why weren't young warriors punished for stealing horses from other Indians?

Teacher: I like this question. It makes me think about the information in the text, but I also use my background knowledge. What did you think about to help you come up with the answer to this question?

Student: I just thought about how my family would react if I stole something. They would be mad. But, I know that horses were really important to the Lakota for survival. So, I guess young warriors weren't punished for stealing horses because they were helping the Lakota to survive.

Teacher: I think you are right. Why do you think this is an author and you question?

Student: Because I had to use my previous experience, and I had to use the information in the text to come up with my answer.

On your own
Why do you think the Lakota would have wars with other Indian tribes?

Teacher: The answer to this question is not in the text, so I will need to consider what I already know about this topic and think for myself.

Figure 5.2. Question Answer Relationships. (Passage quoted above from Santella, A. [2001]. *The Lakota Sioux* [pp. 7–9]. New York, NY: Scholastic Inc.)

more focused when they set purposes for reading than if they are reading just because they are told to do so. Also, asking their own questions about text helps students direct their own reading because searching for an answer requires them to narrow their attention to the most important information needed to answer the question. Because the purpose for reading becomes personal through their own questions, students become self-directed in their pursuit of knowledge. This makes it all the more exciting and supports students' curiosity and interest about their reading. There are many ways to help students learn to develop their own questions. Examples of common approaches are presented next.

Previewing Text Features

Teaching students to preview text features (e.g., pictures, headings, subheadings, captions, bold words) and ask questions that pique interest is one strategy commonly used. A teacher often will write and display students' questions with their names next to them to create a sense of ownership of their own curiosities—something that is especially valuable for struggling readers. A variation of this is to ask students to write their questions on sticky notes. Students feel more motivated to try to find answers once these questions are public and are likely to embark in reading in order to answer them.

This strategy also helps students activate their prior knowledge of the topic. First, the teacher would talk aloud (called *think aloud*) to model identifying specific features in the text. By identifying the text feature, the teacher is modeling the kind of language that students should use when talking about these features. Next, the teacher would ask questions that link what he or she sees in the text to what he or she already knows (his or her prior knowledge). By sharing his or her own questions and wondering aloud about the text feature, a student is able to gain insight into the teacher's cognitive processes and to follow this process in his or her own efforts to develop questions about text. Then, as a way to encourage students to practice previewing text features on their own, the teacher would guide students in making their own connections to the text and generating questions about their reading. When prompting students to generate their own questions, it is important for the teacher to help students find the connections between any relevant background knowledge and the information provided in the text feature. This process is illustrated in Figure 5.3.

The SQ3R (Survey, Question, Read, Recite, Review; Robinson, 1961) is a more formal version of this approach. During the survey step, students preview the text, paying particular attention to headings and text features (e.g., maps, graphs, illustrations). Next, students develop their own questions by rephrasing headings and subheadings as questions. Then, students read the material, taking notes as necessary; recite information that they remember; and review by rereading and checking notes to refresh their memories of the content. This strategy often is used in content area classes such as science and social studies.

Question Frames

Question *rubrics* (also called *frames*) can be used also to teach students how to create text-based questions. When using rubrics, teachers need to emphasize that questions not only have a form but they also have content to which one needs to pay attention. Similar to QAR that is used to help students recognize cognitive demands of existing questions, students can also be taught to categorize their own questions based on the nature of the information they want to ask about. Figure 5.4 is an example of a question rubric with four question levels:

TEACHER: I see a map here, so I am going to look at it closely and read the caption below. It says: "The conquistadors used Hispaniola as a base to explore further into the New World."

I know the New World was the Americas, and this map shows a picture of what is the United States today. I wonder what they were looking for? What questions do you have about the conquistadors and their explorations of the New World?

I would also like to know more about Hispaniola. Can you find it on the map? What other places is it located near?

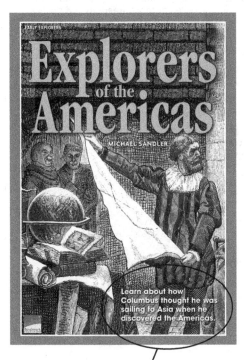

TEACHER: The caption on the cover lets us know what we will be reading about in this book. It says: "Learn about how Columbus thought he was sailing to Asia when he discovered the Americas."

That is interesting, but I still have questions! I wonder why Columbus wanted to go to Asia in the first place? And where was he sailing from?

Can you think of any other questions about Columbus and his journey?

TEACHER: This subheading tells us the name of a person we have not learned about yet: Hernán Cortés.

I have not heard of him before. This is a book about explorers, so I wonder if he is an explorer too? And I wonder if he wanted to sail to Asia like Columbus did?

Before you read this section, what are some things you might want to know about him?

Figure 5.3. Previewing text features to develop questions. (Textbook images from Sandler, M. [2010]. *Explorers of the Americas.* New Rochelle, NY: Benchmark Education Company; reprinted by permission.)

Questioning Rubric

Level 1: Factual information

Questions ask about a simple fact or request a yes/no answer.
Examples:
- How big are sharks?
- Does it get colder at night than during the day when the sun is out?

Level 2: Simple description

Questions ask about a global or general inquiry about a concept rather than a fact. Concepts in a discipline (e.g., adaptation and reproduction are live science concepts; freedom and political upheaval are social studies concepts) need to be previously identified by teachers.
Examples:
- How does the mother shark give birth to the baby shark?
- What do panda bears need to adapt to their environment?

Level 3: Complex explanation

Questions ask for a specific aspect of a concept. These questions look for evidence for an explanation by probing for knowledge or using prior knowledge within the question itself.
Examples:
- Why do most animals that live in the desert come out at night?
- How come llamas have fighting teeth or fangs if they are herbivores?

Level 4: Pattern of relationships

Questions ask about complex interactions or relationships among concepts.
Examples:
- Why do salmon go to the sea to mate and lay their eggs in the river?
- Why do grizzly bears attack humans more often when there is a decline in white bark pines?

Figure 5.4. Questioning rubric. (*Source:* Taboada, & Guthrie, 2006.)

- Level 1: Factual information

- Level 2: Simple description

- Level 3: Complex explanation

- Level 4: Pattern of relationships

These levels can be used explicitly to teach text-based questioning with expository texts in content domains (Taboada & Guthrie, 2004, 2006; Taboada Barber, Richey & Buehl, 2013).

The following guide could be used when teaching questioning and question levels:

1. *Introduce the strategy and explicitly set the purpose.* As with other strategies, it is important for teachers to introduce the strategy and set the purpose for the lesson (see Chapter 7 for specifics on how to explicitly teach strategies). It may be necessary when teaching text-based questions and levels to remind students that good readers ask themselves

questions to help them better understand the text. If we ask ourselves questions, then the meaning becomes clearer. Students might also be reminded to recall their prior knowledge in order to generate questions they have about the text.

2. *Model the use of the strategy.* A way to approach questioning is to have students find the main idea and supporting details in the passage and use these to generate questions. By focusing on the main idea and supporting details, students may be able to create questions that are more relevant and central to the text. A teacher might say the following when modeling this strategy, "Now I am going to identify the main idea and supporting details. Then I am going to try to turn these into questions or curiosities that I have about this book or topic." This might also be a good time to reiterate the importance of asking good questions, rather than trivial or tangential questions to the text (see Chapter 4).

3. *Provide guided practice with the strategy.* As with other strategies, students should have time to demonstrate strategy use with the support of the teacher. They could read the passage independently (or collaboratively), locate the main idea and supporting details or peruse text features, and generate text-based questions. Then, students could share their questions as a class, which provides an opportunity for the teacher to address any student misconceptions regarding question frames as well as determine when students have mastered the strategy.

4. *Provide independent practice with the strategy.* Independent practice is a time for students to demonstrate the newly learned strategy on their own. Students read new text and are prompted to try asking questions while working individually, in pairs, or in small groups. The teacher might scaffold student questions as needed. Overall, this should be a time in which teachers encourage students to be persistent in applying the strategy. Teachers may incorporate exit slips (in which students write a note to the teacher before exiting the class with a description of what they learned or questions that they still have) as a way to assess students' progress and to determine if additional modeling or guided practice is needed.

Teaching students to think about question levels makes them think through the content of the question as well as the type of information needed. In addition, instruction that uses clear levels, or hangers, helps them delve deeper into text (Taboada & Guthrie, 2006; Taboada Barber et al., 2013).

HOW CAN QUESTIONING HELP STUDENTS SUMMARIZE TEXT?

Summarization is a crucial skill for comprehension, but it is extremely challenging for many students, especially when reading large amounts of material. Good readers summarize by putting information they have read into their

NEWS

Armed and Dangerous: Robot Soldiers

A U.S. soldier demonstrates a robot's capabilities at an air base in Afghanistan.

NATIONAL

AT FIRST GLANCE, THE robot looks like a cross between a high-tech toy truck and some kind of space invader. It is four feet tall, rolls around on tractor treads, and has a zoom-lens camera that sticks up like a Cyclops eye. The robot also has a unique feature that will keep it out of the stores: a machine gun that fires real bullets.

What is it? You can call it the Special Weapons Observation Reconnaissance Detection System (SWORDS, for short). If the U.S. military has its way, SWORDS will be among the first in a series of robot soldiers. The Pentagon is set to pour billions of dollars into these mechanical warriors.

"By 2015, we think we can do many missions," Gordon Johnson of the Pentagon's Joint Forces Command told *The New York Times*. "The American military will have these kinds of robots. It's not a question of if, it's a question of when."

Already, robots are digging up bombs in Iraq and serving as scouts and **sentries** [guards] in other locations. Also heading to Iraq is a version of the bomb-disposal robot that fires 1,000 rounds a minute. A soldier with a laptop computer controls the machine.

The $127 billion project, called Future Combat Systems, will develop robots for different functions. Machines will be designed to search buildings and caves, haul weapons, search people, and spy on enemies—as well as shoot. Pentagon officials hope that these robots will help reduce casualties—and cut way down on other human costs.

"They're not afraid," said Johnson. "They don't forget their orders. . . . Will they do a better job than humans? Yes."

But many people raise concerns about using robots as soldiers. Bill Joy, the co-founder of Sun Microsystems, worries that powerful robots could cause "whole new classes of accidents and abuses." Others think that having a "bloodless" army would be a terrible temptation to invade other countries.

What of the basic judgments of logic and morality that every soldier must make? Said one robot maker: "We are a long way from creating a robot that knows what that means."

MARCH 21, 2005 **3**

Figure 5.5. Summarization strategy. (Textbook image from JUNIOR SCHOLASTIC, March 21, 2005. Copyright © 2005 by Scholastic Inc. Sample Summarization Strategy from Regan, K., & Berkeley, S. [2012]. Effective reading and writing instruction: A focus on modeling. *Intervention in School and Clinic, 47,* 278; reprinted by permission.)

Summarization Strategy

Who or what is the sentence/paragraph/section about?

Robot soldiers

What is happening? What are we supposed to learn from this section?

We are supposed to learn about how new technology is being used by the military.

List the most important words from this section (not more than 10)

Robot soldiers
SWORDS (Special Weapons Observation Reconnaissance Detection System)
Pentagon
_By 2015_
Billions (of dollars)
Iraq
Dangerous missions (dig up bombs, serve as scouts and sentries, bomb disposal)
(Save) human casualties
Pros (no fear) and cons (no logic/morality)

Write the main idea of the text (not more than two sentences).

By 2015, the Pentagon plans to spend billions of dollars making robot soldiers called SWORDS to use on dangerous missions in Iraq in hopes to save human casualties. Some think this is a good idea because robots do not show fear, but others think it is a bad idea since robots do not have logic or morality.

own words, which requires them to identify or generate main ideas, make connections among central ideas, discern the most important details, and remember what they read (National Reading Panel, 2000). Explicitly teaching students to summarize can help them to more actively engage in the reading process and understand more of what they read (Gajria & Salvia, 1992; Jitendra, Hoppes, & Xin, 2000). This typically is accomplished by using questioning strategies that help students identify and integrate the most important information. In this chapter, questions embedded within summarization strategies appear in bold font for reader reference. One strategy that can help students summarize text involves three simple steps (Graves, 1986; Jitendra et al., 2000; Malone & Mastropieri, 1992):

1. **Who (or what) is the paragraph about?**

2. **What is happening to the who (or what)?**

3. Create a summary sentence in your own words using less than 10 words.

As noted, the first two steps require student self-questioning. Figure 5.5 shows how a student might use a variation of this strategy to summarize the current events article *Armed and Dangerous: Robot Soldiers* (Scholastic, 2005).

There are other similar strategies designed to help students get the gist of what they are reading. Many of these incorporate questioning as well. For example, the second step in the RAP strategy (Schumaker, Denton, & Deshler, 1984) requires students to self-question:

Read the paragraph.

Ask yourself: What are the main ideas and details of this paragraph?

Put the main ideas and details in your own words.

Similarly, the third step in the TRAVEL strategy (Boyle & Weishaar, 1997) prompts students to self-question:

Topic: Write down the topic.

Read: Read the paragraph.

Ask: Ask what the main idea and three details are and write them down.

Verify: Verify the main idea and linking details.

Examine: Examine the next paragraph and verify again.

Link: When finished, link all of the main ideas.

Understand Your Textbook:
Be a DUCKtective & QRAC the Code!

Question. (Turn headings into questions)

Read. (Read the section and STOP)

Answer. (Ask yourself: Can I answer my question?)

Check. (Check to be sure your answer was correct OR summarize the section)

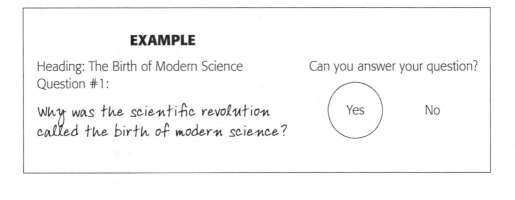

EXAMPLE

Heading: The Birth of Modern Science
Question #1:

Why was the scientific revolution called the birth of modern science?

Can you answer your question?

Yes   No

Need More Clues?

- Did you understand the <u>vocabulary</u>? *Look for the definition of bold words.*
- Were there clues in the <u>text features</u>? *Study maps and graphs.*
- Do you know anything else about the topic? *Use your prior knowledge.*
- Was your question not answered? *Try to summarize the section instead!*
  - Who was the section about?
  - What happened in the section?
  - Tell what the section was about in less than 2 sentences.
- Really really stuck? *Re-read the section and try again!*

Figure 5.6. QRAC-the-Code strategy. (From Berkeley, S., & Riccomini, P. J. [2013]. QRAC-the-Code: A comprehension monitoring strategy for middle school social studies textbooks. *Journal of Learning Disabilities, 46,* 154–165; reprinted by permission.)

The QRAC-the-Code strategy (Berkeley & Riccomini, 2013) prompts students to ask questions (step 1) and later answer those questions (step 3):

1. **Question (turn headings into questions)**
2. Read (read the section and stop)
3. **Answer (ask yourself: "Can I answer my question?")**
4. Check (check to be sure your answer was correct or summarize the section)

Notice how many strategies employ a mnemonic to assist students in remembering the steps to the reading strategy (see Chapter 3). In addition, strategies often include some sort of visual reminder to help students remember each of the steps. Figure 5.6 is a strategy sheet for the QRAC-the-Code strategy. In addition, Chapter 7 includes a scripted modeling lesson for this strategy.

Other strategies lend themselves to using question frames. Collaborative Strategic Reading (CSR; e.g., Klingner, Vaughn, & Schumm, 1998) is one example. CSR utilizes cooperative learning in the following areas: 1) previewing (activating prior knowledge), 2) "click and clunk" (comprehension monitoring), 3) getting the gist (summarizing with self-questioning), and 4) wrap-up (content-specific self-questioning). The following question frames can be used within CSR to assist students in forming appropriate questions within the wrap-up:

- How were ____ and ____ the same? Different?
- What do you think would happen if ____?
- What do you think caused ____ to happen?
- What other solution can you think of for the problem of ____?
- What might have prevented the problem of ____ from happening?
- What are the strengths (or weaknesses) of ____? (Klingner & Vaughn, 1998, p. 34)

In addition, students can be taught content free questions that can generalize across texts (see Chapter 6 for more on content free questions).

WHAT CHALLENGES MIGHT ARISE RELATED TO QUESTIONING?

Students who struggle to comprehend what they read often fail to engage with text in meaningful ways. Asking and answering questions while reading promotes this important engagement. In fact, questioning, and self-questioning in particular, has been well documented to help students improve reading comprehension (Berkeley, Scruggs, & Mastropieri, 2010; Gersten et al., 2001). There are some considerations for teachers to keep in mind when teaching students to question because this is a challenging task for many students and especially students with learning disabilities (LD) and those who are English language learners (ELLs).

Caution 1

Some students will need additional time to think (called *think time*) when answering questions. For ELLs, answering questions in class can be daunting (Alvermann et al., 2010). Depending on their English proficiency, they may need extra time to process text information in order to formulate and answer questions. This is also the case for students with LD who often incorrectly answer questions and are afraid to be embarrassed in front of their peers. To help mitigate these potential difficulties, teachers can be very intentional when asking questions in class. Consider Mrs. Jones' approach:

Mrs. Jones: World War II had been going on for some time, but the United States did not get involved right away. What event happened that made the United States decide to become involved in World War II? Matthew, I am going to ask you to answer that question for me in just a few minutes. But first, Steve, can you remind me who the axis powers were?

Steve: Japan, Italy, and Germany.

Mrs. Jones: That is right. And what were the two countries allied with the United States? Sarah?

Sarah: Great Britain and Russia.

Mrs. Jones: Matthew, what event caused the United States to decide to become involved in World War II?

Matthew: Pearl Harbor.

Mrs. Jones: What happened at Pearl Harbor?

Matthew: Japan bombed Pearl Harbor.

Mrs. Jones: So why would the United States care about that? Where is Pearl Harbor?

Matthew: Pearl Harbor is in Hawaii. Plus, the attack destroyed a lot of U.S. ships and soldiers, so the United States probably wanted to fight back.

Mrs. Jones: Nice job using what you read and what you already know to think through the answer to the question!

Notice in this scenario that Mrs. Jones lets Matthew know that she would be calling on him to answer a specific question so that he had time to think about his answer. She also asks follow-up questions to help elicit more information and determine his level of understanding of the concepts. This would be especially important if Matthew was not originally from the United States and might not know that Hawaii is a state and that Pearl Harbor is a military port. Finally, she gives feedback that reinforces the student's process for thinking through the answer; in this way, she makes the hidden act of comprehension visible to the others in the class.

⚠ Caution 2

The idea that students should be encouraged to ask and answer questions while reading appears rather straightforward. Although many students will easily pick this up, others will not. Some students have difficulty independently generating questions, particularly if they have LD or are ELLs. For example, students may make up questions that are too broad or too narrow.

Some students will create questions that are so far off topic that they cannot be answered in the reading. Think about the current events article *Armed and Dangerous: Robot Soldiers* from earlier in this chapter. A student might preview an illustration within the article of a soldier standing by the SWORDS robot and ask, "How are robots built?" Although this is a reasonable question, it will not help the student understand this particular passage because it is about how the robots are used by the military and not how they are designed and built.

Conversely, a student struggling to ask meaningful questions may ask ones that are too specific and irrelevant to understanding the main ideas of the text. This student might skim ahead to find information written word for word within an individual sentence and base his or her question on this answer before he or she ever begins reading. For example, a student reading *Armed and Dangerous: Robot Soldiers* might skim ahead and ask

- What year will we be able to do missions? or

- How much money was spent making robots?

By asking questions such as these, the student who is self-conscious about giving an incorrect answer is assured of being correct. Although this student will be able to answer these specific questions, this will not help him or her understand the broader meaning of the text. This type of student will need additional assistance with creating meaningful questions.

Preteaching of skills is necessary when working with such students; simply prompting students to ask questions will not be sufficient. Instead, teachers should explicitly teach students question stems (Who? What? Where? When? Why? How?) and question frames. Furthermore, teachers should ensure that students know how to grammatically form questions (see Chapter 1). Providing supports for students in creating questions can alleviate their anxiety about the question *form* so they can focus more on the *content* of the question and engage more meaningfully with text.

These same students also are likely to have difficulty persisting with strategy use when reading large amounts of text because it takes them longer to develop questions to answer while they are reading. Therefore, particularly when students are mastering how to form appropriate questions to assist with reading comprehension, it is important for teachers to assign texts at a level that students can read independently (or with minimum scaffolding) so they can sustain interest and ask relevant questions about text. In addition, it may be good to give students extra time to discuss their questions with classmates in small groups. For some ELLs, encouraging them to ask questions in their first language (L1) may also be helpful. This extra time will allow students to think through the content, formulate the questions in their minds, and use question form to pose them orally. If time is too brief, then students may have questions in their minds that they are unable to articulate. The ultimate goal of having students ask text-related questions before, during, and after reading is to have students connect with the text, answer their questions, and continue to read if their questions go unanswered.

WHAT ELSE DO TEACHERS NEED TO KNOW ABOUT QUESTIONING?

Questioning plays an important role throughout the reading process. For example, before reading, students might ask themselves questions about what they already know about the topic, what the purpose of their reading will be, and what type of text they will be reading. During reading, asking and answering questions can help students interact with the text and monitor when comprehension has broken down. After reading, questions can help students summarize and synthesize this new information they have read with what they already know about the topic. Questioning strategies have been shown to help students understand more of what they read, regardless of the purpose of the questions. The ultimate goal of questioning strategy instructions is to help students ask and answer appropriate questions throughout the reading process because this has been show to improve reading comprehension. Chapter 7 contains information on how to teach students to read strategically and why this is important for learning.

6

Teach Students to Recognize Text Structure

There are two primary types of text—narrative and expository. Reading comprehension strategies vary in utility depending on the type of text being read. Knowledge of text structure in and of itself can support reading comprehension. In addition, visual representations of text structures that connect ideas found in text (e.g., story maps, graphic organizers) can assist students with reading comprehension.

WHAT IS TEXT STRUCTURE AND WHY IS IT IMPORTANT FOR READING COMPREHENSION?

Chapter 2 discussed how all texts are not written at the same difficulty level. Similarly, all texts do not present information in the same format. There are two primary types of text:

- Narrative (fiction)

- Expository/informational (nonfiction)

In addition to having different presentation formats (called *text structures*), these types of texts have different purposes. The primary purpose of narrative text is to tell a story or entertain, whereas the primary purpose of expository text is to inform, explain, or persuade. Both types of text encompass a wide range of genres. Table 6.1 compares and contrasts the common characteristics of these types of text.

As with all reading strategies, understanding text structure is a tool for students to use to help them comprehend, not an end goal in and of itself (Calkins, 2001; Institute of Education Sciences, 2010). "Text structure instruction makes the invisible visible so readers can use the content and the structure of the text itself as a tool to enhance understanding, to manipulate their thinking, and revise their existing knowledge, beliefs, and feelings" (Keene, 2008, p. 179).

Table 6.1. Characteristics of narrative versus expository texts

	Narrative text	Expository text
Example genres	Novels, short stories, folktales, tall tales, myths, fables, legends, fantasies	Textbooks, biographies, newspapers/ magazines, how-to texts (e.g., recipes, manuals, brochures)
Typical structure	Story grammar (character, setting, conflict, resolution)	Temporal (time or order sequences), descriptive (or definition/example), collection (listing), compare and contrast, cause and effect (or problem and solution)
Text features	Title, chapters, illustrations (in picture books)	Table of contents; preface; chapter introductions; chapter headings and subheadings; marginal notes; chapter summaries; maps, charts, graphs, and illustrations; index; glossary
Characteristics	Written in language that is similar to spoken language in style; familiar ideas with themes that often connect to reader's experiences	Formal language with large numbers of vocabulary terms that may be unfamiliar to the reader; highly technical, multisyllabic words; structural complexity and variety and information density; reader often may not have background knowledge; varies in writing style (persuasion, how to, informative)

This process of making the text structure overt helps students extract and construct meaning while reading (Jitendra & Gajria, 2011). Furthermore, students are more likely to use other appropriate strategies to help gain meaning from text (e.g., activating prior knowledge, previewing the text, setting a purpose for reading) when they recognize the structure of the text (Denton et al., 2012).

WHAT INSTRUCTIONAL TECHNIQUES CAN HELP STUDENTS UNDERSTAND NARRATIVE TEXT?

Most children already have an ear for traditional story structure when they enter school (Dymock, 2007; Keene, 2008). Those children who have been read to as babies or toddlers are aware that there is a character that has a problem or a challenge that he or she works to solve until things come to a climax, and then everything turns out well in the end. It is this understanding of story structure that helps readers make predictions about what will come next, anticipate character development, and summarize the story (Baumann & Bergeron, 1993; Calkins, 2001). Although many students enter school with a general understanding of how stories go, not all students have this prior experience. There are students for whom oral storytelling or reading has not been commonplace in their home. Also, narrative story plots become more complex with flashbacks, subplots, and alternating points of view as students progress through the grades. An understanding of basic story structure will not carry all students through these more complex and subtler stories, and explicit instruction on story structure will be needed.

It is well documented that direct instruction in the component parts of story structures can help students understand more of what they read (Duke & Pearson, 2002; Fisher, Frey, & Lapp, 2008; Pearson & Cervetti, 2012). Although not all components of narrative text structure are agreed upon by literacy experts, characters, setting, and plot are widely accepted as key elements of a story (Fountas, 2001; Keene, 2008). Other possible narrative text elements include theme, perspective, antagonist, protagonist, movement through time, change, goals, conflict, rising action, climax, falling action, and resolution. These features are often referred to as *story grammar.*

Using Story Maps to Better Understand Narrative Text

One way that teachers can help students to recognize the important elements of the narrative is through visual representations of the story structure (Dymock, 2007; Fountas, 2001; Institute of Education Sciences, 2010). Although not the only type of display, the story map is perhaps the most commonly used visual representation of narrative text. Figures 6.1, 6.2, and 6.3 are examples of story maps that range in complexity. The first might be used when story grammar is first being introduced (typically in elementary school grades), the second might be used as students gain proficiency, and the third might be used as narratives become more advanced conceptually (typically in secondary levels).

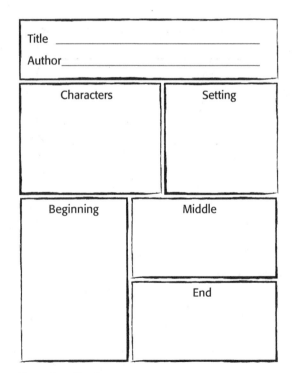

Figure 6.1. Simple story map.

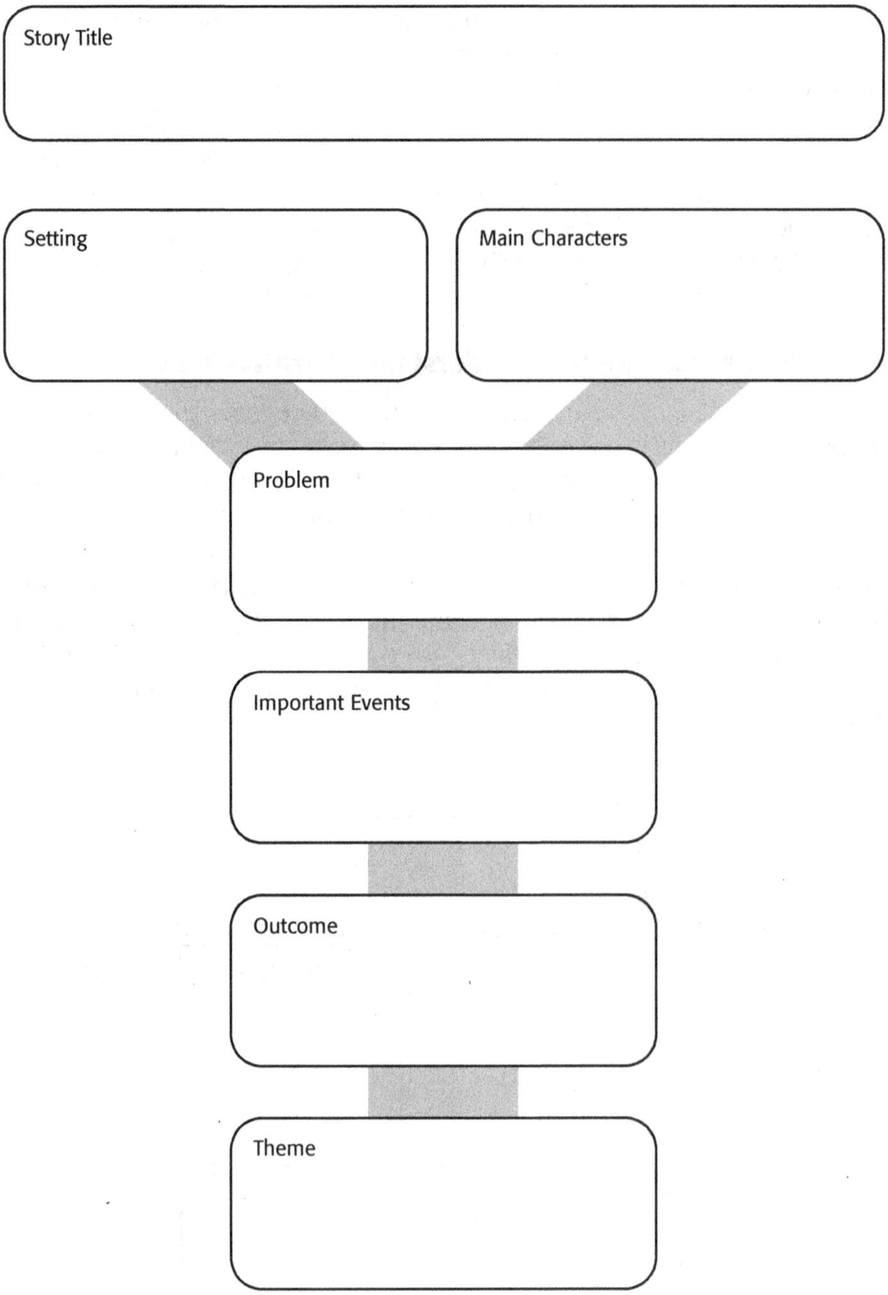

Story Title

Setting

Main Characters

Problem

Important Events

Outcome

Theme

Figure 6.2. Intermediate story map.

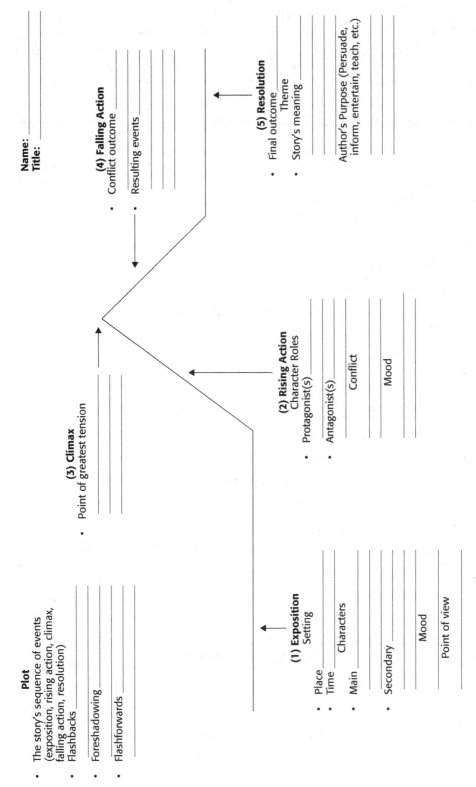

Name: _____
Title: _____

Plot
- The story's sequence of events (exposition, rising action, climax, falling action, resolution)
- Flashbacks _____
- Foreshadowing _____
- Flashforwards _____

(3) Climax
- Point of greatest tension

(4) Falling Action
- Conflict outcome _____
- Resulting events _____
_____
_____
_____

(5) Resolution
- Final outcome _____
- Theme _____
- Story's meaning _____

Author's Purpose (Persuade, inform, entertain, teach, etc.)
_____
_____

(2) Rising Action
Character Roles
- Protagonist(s) _____
- Antagonist(s) _____
Conflict _____
Mood _____

(1) Exposition
Setting
- Place _____
- Time _____
- Characters
  Main _____
- Secondary _____
Mood _____
Point of view _____

Figure 6.3. Advanced story map.

87

Alternatively, the same story map can be used with differentiated texts in which the teacher models the use of the story map, then provides supported guided practice, and finally students apply what they learn with a grade-level narrative. Text Box 6.1 illustrates how this practice can be used within instruction.

Asking and Answering Questions to Better Understand Narrative Text

In addition to using story maps, it also may be helpful to teach students *content free* questions that they can ask while reading narrative texts (Jennings et al., 2010). These questions are not topic specific, but rather can be asked across texts to help the reader interact with the story. Following are questions based on narrative story structure (Caldwell & Leslie, 2005):

- Who is the main character? Why do you think so?
- Who are other important characters? Why are they important?
- What is the character's problem?
- How is the character trying to solve his or her problem?
- How is the setting important to the story?
- What do I predict will happen next? Why do I think so?
- Do I agree or disagree with what the character did? Why?
- Do I like or dislike this part of the story? Why?
- Is this story true to life? Why or why not? How did the story end?
- Is there anything I don't understand?
- What surprised me about this story?
- If I were going to write the author, what would I say?

Notice that there are dual goals for these questions. First, content free questions prompt the reader to recognize the story grammar elements (e.g., character, setting, events) inherent to narrative text structures. Second, these questions help students think more deeply about the content. Look again at the questions. Which ones help the students recognize text structure? Which help the student think more deeply about the content? Which do both?

WHAT INSTRUCTIONAL TECHNIQUES CAN HELP STUDENTS UNDERSTAND EXPOSITORY TEXT?

Numerous forms of *expository text* (also referred to as *informational text*) are available; however, textbooks are perhaps the most heavily emphasized in content area classes beginning in the fourth grade because teachers rely on these texts as instructional tools to address state curriculum standards (Vidal-Abarca, Martinez, & Gilabert, 2000).

(continued on page 94)

Text Box 6.1

PRACTICAL APPLICATION

Scaffolded Instruction in Practice

Kelly Liu is a middle school special education teacher. The following is her description of how she scaffolds instruction in narrative text structure and story grammar elements for students in her language arts classes. Figures 6.4–6.6 illustrate how this practice can be used within instruction.

"How many of you like roller coasters?" That is how I introduce the subject of *plot* to my students. Most of the kids will raise their hands, get excited, and start talking all at once comparing roller coaster rides. The ones that do not like roller coasters will say so and argue why they do not like them. I know at this point that their attention is on roller coasters.

"Well, plot is a lot like a roller coaster." I explain to them that the best part about the ride is the buildup of excitement as you climb up and up and up on a roller coaster. Once you reach the top and are just about to go over, your heart is pounding so hard all you can do as you go over the crest is scream for release, and then it is all over before you know it. This metaphor is something I know they can relate to, and I will repeatedly use it throughout the fiction unit. The climb up on a coaster is the *rising action* to a story; everything starts to build up. The crest at the top is the *climax*; "it is that moment, like the stretching of a rubber band, where you just do not know when it is going to break; then whoa! You are going over the top and falling." This is the *falling action* to a story; it is quick and short as you roll to a stop at the end—the *resolution.*

I play up the roller coaster ride as I regale them with this metaphor. I am perched on a stool in the front of the room. I use my body to mimic the actions of going up a roller coaster, leaning as far back as I can and even include broad facial contortions. I make my voice loud and screechy as I suddenly lean forward and mimic the downward rush. The students love it—and I have succeeded in my goal to capture their interest.

Making connections is one of the most important ways for students with learning disabilities to understand difficult concepts within the curriculum. I intentionally attempt to help students make these connections. For example, I might bring up the movie *Spiderman* because most of them have seen it. I explain that Spiderman is the *protagonist*, the good guy. When I ask who the *antagonist* is, they know it is the Green Goblin. We talk about the run-ins that Spiderman has with the Green Goblin (what happens, who was involved) and this discussion leads them to the climax. "When is Spiderman's *conflict* with the Green Goblin over?" Of course they know it is when the Green Goblin dies. I tell them that the moment right before he dies is the climax to the story. Spiderman is pretty beat up, we do not know what is going to happen or who will win the battle, and just when we think Spiderman is going to die, something happens and Green Goblin gets it instead. I explain that it is the moment right before the main conflict is over that we have reached the climax to the story. They understand this quite well.

To get them started on plotting the narrative story elements on a diagram, I use a simple story like *Cinderella.* We go through the story; we read a short version of the story, and I model for them how to fill in a plot diagram to visually display the narrative text structure (see Figure 6.4). I start with the *exposition*. "Who are the main characters?" I say aloud and answer aloud as I fill in the information. I go through each part aloud, and they often like to answer me as I pose questions to myself aloud. When I get to the climax, I ask myself aloud, "Let's see, when does the main conflict end?" I pinpoint it to when we know Cinderella no longer has to live with the stepfamily and that is when her foot goes into the shoe. That is when the prince learns she is the one from the ball and says that she is to become his princess. I say out loud that I need to find the moment right before then—that is the greatest moment of tension, and that is when the prince approaches her to try on the shoe.

When it is time for them to try to fill in the story plot on their own, I choose a short story by Rudyard Kipling, *Rikki Tikki Tavi*. Like *Cinderella*, it has colorful characters, is a simple story, and has a clear conflict. I have them listen to the story, follow along in the book, and make note of important facts about setting and main characters. I ask them to visualize the story as they listen and write down any questions they may have as to what is going on if they get confused. We fill out the diagram together when they have heard the story, and I support them by supplying information they missed or misinterpreted (see Figure 6.5). I ask them what they think should go next until we reach the climax to the story. Again, I ask the question, "When does the main conflict end?" After a couple attempts and my asking them the same question in different ways, narrowing the action to the point they are trying to get to, the answer comes out: when Rikki goes into the snake hole after Nagaina. I explain to them that at that moment we do not know who will win in the snake hole. The story tells them that "very few mongooses, however wise and old they may be, care to follow a cobra into its hole." If they do not understand why, then I explain it to them.

We use the book *Freak the Mighty* by Rodman Philbrick when it is time for them to show me what they have learned. This grade-level text is quite challenging because the students in my class are all struggling readers. I read the story to them, acting out with voices and drama. They love the story for its characters. We take notes throughout the reading that will be used to help them develop their plot diagrams (see Figure 6.6). This story is a full chapter book and it takes some time to work through all the areas required based on the curriculum, but I keep the plot diagram information central to our conversations. I have broken down the chapters designed to assist with filling in their plot diagrams, so when something happens I ask aloud, "Does this sound like something that should go into the diagram?" Every now and then I will throw a curve ball to see if they understand the difference between what sounds good and what is necessary or essential to the plot.

Every day we pick up on the story. I review what we have read and ask them about conflict. The main character goes through many conflicts and transformations and this can get very confusing. Differentiating between main conflict and general conflicts is one of the hardest things for my students to do. We make a list of the different types of conflicts we encounter along the way, which serves two purposes. First, they learn by example the different types of conflict that can be found in a story and how these conflicts are applied in text. Second, they have to question as they read (good reading strategy) if it involves the main character so they do not lose sight of the main conflict.

Plot diagram
Cinderella

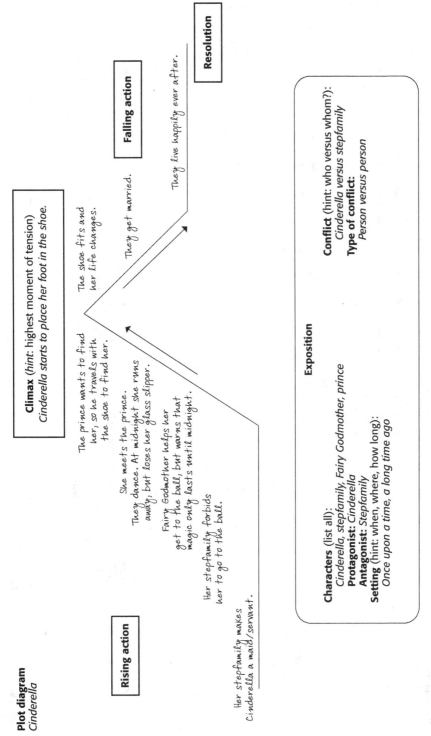

Rising action

Her stepfamily makes
Cinderella a maid/servant.

Her stepfamily forbids
her to go to the ball.

Fairy Godmother helps her
get to the ball, but warns that
magic only lasts until midnight.

She meets the prince.
They dance. At midnight she runs
away, but loses her glass slipper.

Climax (*hint:* highest moment of tension)
Cinderella starts to place her foot in the shoe.

The prince wants to find
her, so he travels with
the shoe to find her.

The shoe fits and
her life changes.

Falling action

They get married.

They live happily ever after.

Resolution

Exposition

Characters (list all):
Cinderella, stepfamily, Fairy Godmother, prince
Protagonist: *Cinderella*
Antagonist: *Stepfamily*
Setting (hint: when, where, how long):
Once upon a time, a long time ago

Conflict (hint: who versus whom?):
Cinderella versus stepfamily
Type of conflict:
Person versus person

Figure 6.4. Story map for *Cinderella*.

Plot diagram
Rikki Tikki Tavi

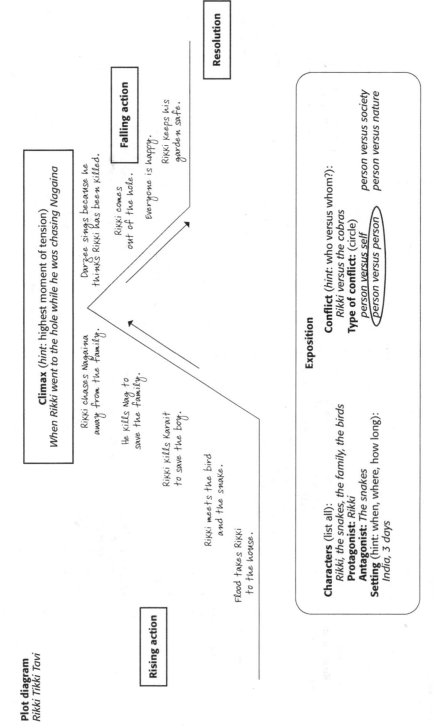

Rising action

Flood takes Rikki to the house.

Rikki meets the bird and the snake.

Rikki kills Karait to save the boy.

He kills Nag to save the family.

Rikki chases Nagaina away from the family.

Climax (*hint:* highest moment of tension)
When Rikki went to the hole while he was chasing Nagaina

Falling action

Darzee sings because he thinks Rikki has been killed.

Rikki comes out of the hole.

Everyone is happy.

Rikki keeps his garden safe.

Resolution

Exposition

Characters (list all):
Rikki, the snakes, the family, the birds
Protagonist: *Rikki*
Antagonist: *The snakes*
Setting (hint: when, where, how long):
India, 3 days

Conflict (*hint:* who versus whom?):
Rikki versus the cobras
Type of conflict: (circle)
person versus self   person versus society
Person versus person   person versus nature

Figure 6.5.   Story map for *Rikki Tikki Tavi*.

Plot diagram
Freak the Mighty

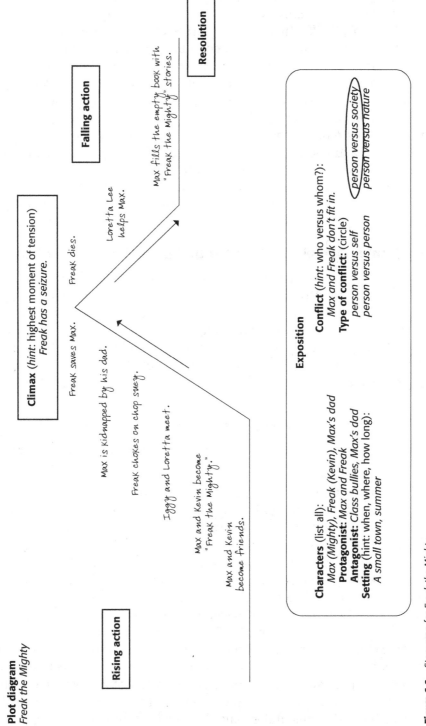

Rising action

Climax (*hint:* highest moment of tension)
Freak has a seizure.

Freak saves Max.   Freak dies.

Falling action

Resolution

Max is kidnapped by his dad.

Freak chokes on chop suey.

Iggy and Loretta meet.

Max and Kevin become "Freak the Mighty."

Max and Kevin become friends.

Loretta Lee helps Max.

Max fills the empty book with "Freak the Mighty" stories.

Exposition

Characters (list all):
Max (Mighty), Freak (Kevin), Max's dad
Protagonist: *Max and Freak*
Antagonist: *Class bullies, Max's dad*
Setting (hint: when, where, how long):
A small town, summer

Conflict (*hint:* who versus whom?):
Max and Freak don't fit in.
Type of conflict: (circle)
person versus self
person versus person
person versus society
person versus nature

Figure 6.6.   Story map for *Freak the Mighty*.

Acquiring new knowledge from the textbook is a significant academic challenge for many students (Hall, 2004; Lovitt & Horton, 1994). This is in large part because of the varied text structure, conceptual density, and large numbers of unfamiliar vocabulary terms that are found in textbooks (Saenz & Fuchs, 2002). In addition, textbooks often are written far above the students' actual grade level and contain large numbers of multisyllabic words that are difficult for students to decode and understand. Finally, textbooks are even organized "inconsiderately"—in such a way that it is difficult for readers to anticipate how to approach the text (Harniss, Dickson, Kinder, & Hollenbeck, 2001). The structure of the text (and the relationship of concepts represented) can vary from chapter to chapter, paragraph to paragraph, and even sentence to sentence (Berkeley, King-Sears, Hott, & Bradley-Black, 2014). For example, within the same chapter, one section may convey cause/effect relationships, the next might convey a temporal sequence, and yet another may provide a description of an important term or concept.

Using Graphic Organizers to Better Understand Expository Text

Graphic organizers are visual representations of text that help with understanding of information by showing how information about the topic is organized (Ellis & Howard, 2007). Graphic organizers can be used to help students activate background knowledge (see Chapter 4), develop vocabulary knowledge (see Chapter 3), and serve as advanced organizers for reading to help students better understand the relationship between and among concepts.

"A picture is worth a thousand words."

Arthur Brisbane, American newspaper editor

The previous section illustrated how specific types of graphic organizers (story maps) can help students comprehend narrative text. Although there are many versions of story maps, the function is consistent—to help students recognize narrative text structure as a way to help them anticipate and understand what they are reading. This becomes more complex, however, when reading expository text because a single expository text is likely to contain a wide range of text structures. Graphic organizers visually display information so that related facts and concepts within the text are more apparent (Gajria, Jitendra, Sood, & Sacks, 2007; Kim, Vaughn, Wanzek, & Wei, 2004). For example, if the main point of the text was to help students have a firmer understanding of types of governments, then a Venn diagram could be used to visually compare and contrast the characteristics of democracy (a known concept) and totalitarianism (a new concept). If the main focus of the reading task was to help students understand the steps that are needed to complete a science experiment, then a graphic organizer that represents the order of the experiment steps would be beneficial. In the first example, a visual representation helps students understand that they should focus on information related to similarities and differences (in other words, compare and contrast text structure) between forms of government. In the second example, the visual representation of the graphic organizer helps students understand that attending to the order of steps (temporal text structure) is important for comprehension. Graphic organizers can also help students learn definitions of important terms (see Chapter 3).

Graphic organizers can take a large number of forms (see Table 6.2 for resources) so the critical consideration for instruction is to intentionally select organizers that match the text that the students are reading and accurately represent both the primary concepts that students should understand and the relationships between/among those concepts. In other words, it is important for teachers to preread text to determine how well the graphic organizer will support student comprehension. Figures 6.7, 6.8, and 6.9 illustrate this point. Furthermore, if different students are reading different texts, then they may not all be able to use the same graphic organizer. Eventually, students should be taught to independently identify text structure and appropriate graphic organizers. In a study on teachers' perceptions on the value of text structure, a teacher remarked how she taught students to select graphic organizers based on the text structure:

> I was trying to have students complete graphic organizers after they had read something. I realized that they didn't know what to record or which tool to use. I could have just copied the correct graphic organizer, but then they wouldn't learn about the text. I now explain the text structure and how I know which structure the author has used. Then I model a sample graphic organizer to collect my information. My students have learned to do this on their own—they determine which graphic organizers to use because they're looking for the implicit structure of the text. (Fisher et al., 2008, p. 554)

Table 6.2. Graphic organizer template resources

Adolescent Literacy (http://www.adlit.org): Many templates for narrative and expository text are available, including KWL, jigsaw, anticipation guides, and summarization.

Reading Rockets (http://www.readingrockets.org): Story maps and graphic organizers for a variety of genres and purposes are available. Many of them can be found in the strategy section of the website; however, examples and templates are also embedded in articles.

Houghton Mifflin Harcourt Education Place (http://www.eduplace.com): A wide variety of graphic organizers to structure writing and assist with problem solving, planning, and brainstorming are available.

Scholastic (http://www.scholastic.com): Graphic organizers on this site are categorized by grade level and type (organizer patterns, reading comprehension, and story elements). Some items are free, and others only can be accessed if you are a subscriber.

Florida Center for Reading Research (http://www.fcrr.org): A wide array of lesson plans using graphic organizers are available through the student center activities section of the web site. They can be accessed through the search engine on the web site.

edHelper.com (http://edhelper.com/teachers/graphic_organizers.htm): Organizers on this site include Venn diagrams, concept maps, and reading and writing graphic organizers

Some flowers are chooosy about whom they invite for dinner. They have such an unusual shape that only one species of animal can feed from them. Madagascar star orchids grow tubes up to 11 inches (28 cm) deep. Nectar collects at the bottom of the tubes. Nothing can reach this nectar except a type of hawk moth. The moth's proboscis extends up to four times the length of its body. The flower cannot reproduce without the hawk moth, while the moth cannot feed on any other plant.

Flowers such as the pink gentian have particulary fine pollen. When a visiting carpenter bee lands on the flower, it vibrates its wings at a very precise speed. This dislodges the pollen from the flower. Only the carpenter bee can gain access to the flower's pollen.

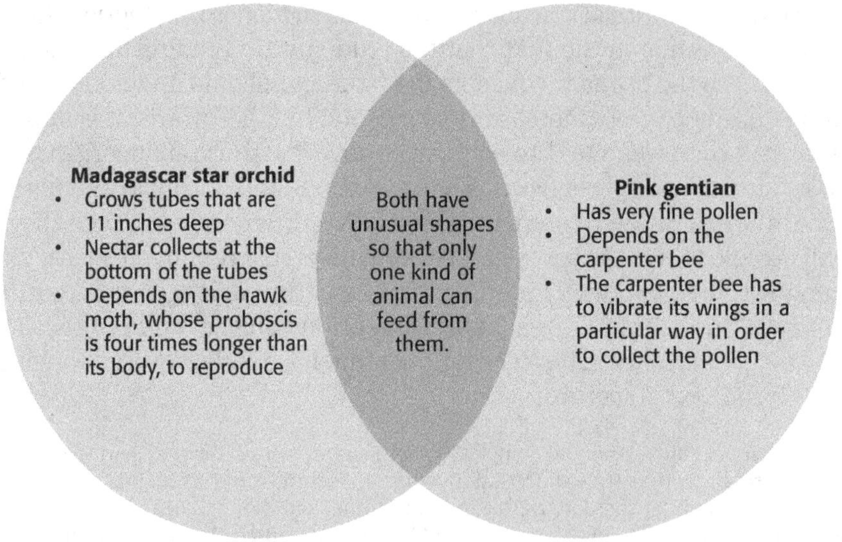

Madagascar star orchid
- Grows tubes that are 11 inches deep
- Nectar collects at the bottom of the tubes
- Depends on the hawk moth, whose proboscis is four times longer than its body, to reproduce

Both have unusual shapes so that only one kind of animal can feed from them.

Pink gentian
- Has very fine pollen
- Depends on the carpenter bee
- The carpenter bee has to vibrate its wings in a particular way in order to collect the pollen

Figure 6.7. Compare and contrast text structure example. (Passage quoted above from Hoare, B. [2003]. *Parasites and partners: Breeders.* Chicago, IL: Heinemann-Raintree.)

Once students have learned to identify text structure and an appropriate corresponding graphic organizer, a strategy such as POSSE (Englert & Mariage, 1991) may be a helpful next step. The steps to POSSE are

1. <u>P</u>redict text ideas based on prior knowledge.

2. <u>O</u>rganize predicted text ideas and prior knowledge in a graphic organizer.

3. **<u>S</u>earch for the text structure.**

4. <u>S</u>ummarize main ideas and record on the organizer.

5. <u>E</u>valuate comprehension, ask questions, and predict what information will be presented next.

Asking and Answering Questions to Better Understand Expository Text

As with narrative text, it also may be helpful to teach students *content free* questions that they can ask when reading expository texts (Jennings et al.,

2010). However, instead of asking content free questions that relate to story grammar, these content free questions should lend themselves to informational (expository) text. The KWL chart is a strategy that lends itself to questioning with expository texts (see Chapter 4). Before reading, students ask themselves, "*What do I already know about this topic?*" and "*What do I want to know?*" Then, after reading, they ask themselves, "*What did I*

> Giant pandas are one of the most popular animals in the world. But they are in danger. Hunters sell them, so there are not many left.
>
> Giant pandas eat mostly bamboo shoots. Because people have moved into the land where bamboo grows, the pandas now have a hard time finding food. Pandas have less food because people are chopping down more bamboo.

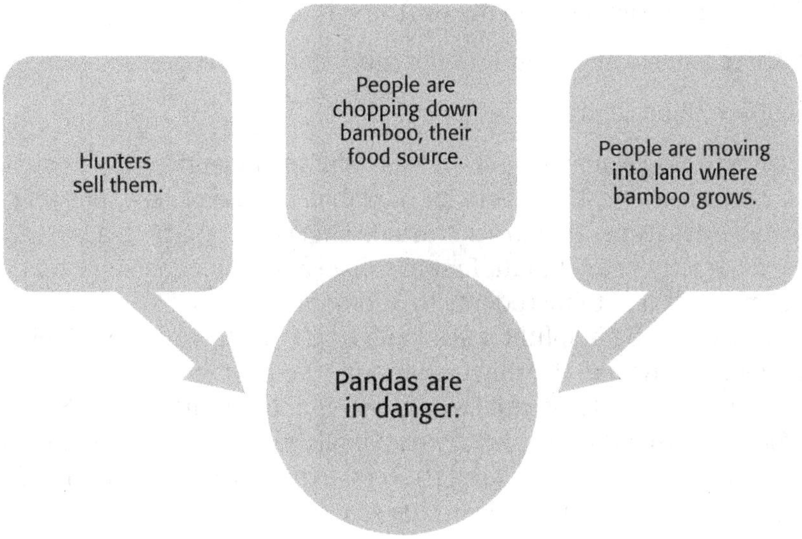

Hunters sell them.

People are chopping down bamboo, their food source.

People are moving into land where bamboo grows.

Pandas are in danger.

Figure 6.8. Cause and effect text structure example. (Passage quoted above from Thompson, G. [1998]. *Animals in danger*. Austin, TX: Steck-Vaughn.)

> We drifted into the center of the cloud. Ms. Frizzle was right—it was damp in there. The cloud was made of tiny water droplets hanging in the air. Inside the cloud, droplets began coming together. They formed bigger and bigger drops. As the drops became heavier, they started falling.

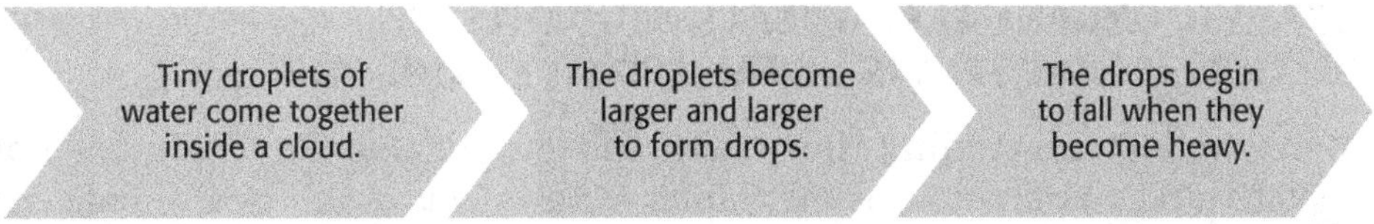

Tiny droplets of water come together inside a cloud.

The droplets become larger and larger to form drops.

The drops begin to fall when they become heavy.

Figure 6.9. Temporal text structure. (Passage quoted above from Cole, J., & Degan, B. [1995]. *The magic school bus: Inside a hurricane*. New York, NY: Scholastic Inc.)

learn?" These content free questions can help students activate their prior knowledge of the topic, set a purpose for reading, and answer questions about their reading. Following are additional content free questions that are appropriate for expository story structure (Caldwell & Leslie, 2005):

- What is the topic of this section?

- What is the author's purpose in writing this selection?

- What are the most important ideas?

- What did I learn?

- What do I already know about this?

- How is this different from what I already knew?

- What surprised me?

- How could I explain this in my own words?

- What are some words that I do not know the meaning of?

- What don't I understand?

As you can see, these questions are not as helpful for identifying text structure as the content free questions were for narrative text because expository texts tend to have structures that are so varied. This is part of the reason why narrative text structures are taught first in school and why expository text structures are more difficult for students to understand. Regardless, these content free questions can be helpful for students to get them started with checking their understanding and digging deeper into the meaning of the text.

Content free questions can be so broad in focus that they may be appropriate for use with either expository or narrative forms of text. For example, Chapter 5 introduced a questioning strategy to help students summarize their reading. A variation of questions in this strategy are

- Who (or what) is this text about?

- What is happening to the who (or what)?

- Write a summary of what you read in two sentences.

Because this summarization strategy is broad, it could be used with either type of text.

WHAT ARE POTENTIAL PROBLEMS WHEN USING GRAPHIC ORGANIZERS TO TEACH STUDENTS TO RECOGNIZE HOW TEXT IS ORGANIZED (TEXT STRUCTURE)?

Many students, including those with learning disabilities (LD), are not sensitive to text structures (Williams, 1998). This is an area of concern because research has shown that students understand more of what they read when they are explicitly taught to recognize how text is organized (i.e., the text structure; e.g., Broer, Aarnoutse, Kieviet, & Van Leeuwe, 2002; Gunn, 2008; Meyer & Ray, 2011). We are beginning to have a better understanding, however, of how to help these students to be more cognizant of the way that text is structured (Mastropieri & Scruggs, 1997). For example, graphic organizers often are used in instruction because they enable facts and concepts to be visually represented in a concrete manner, which allows difficult material to be scaffolded for a range of student learners (Gajria et al., 2007; Griffin & Tulbert, 1995). Yet, there are some cautions for which teachers should be aware.

⚠ Caution 1

Do not assume students have knowledge of text structures or that they automatically make connections (see Chapter 4); this is not always the case—particularly for students with LD or who are English language learners (ELL; Nagy, 1997; Pace et al., 1989). Be sure to select graphic organizers that are appropriate for the type of text and/or text structure and that students are explicitly taught to recognize the relationship between concepts represented. Eventually, students need to own the process of recognizing text structure to facilitate their comprehension, so it is extremely important to provide sufficient modeling and practice until they are proficient. Failure to do so will impede future use of the strategy by students. See Chapter 7 for more information about how to effectively teach strategies.

It is important to remember that graphic organizers are intended to assist students with recognizing the way a text is organized so they can learn more about the content of the text through simultaneous understanding of its structure. Learning about structure is not an end in itself and it does not come naturally. Indeed, even though most students have had experiences with oral and narrative texts since early ages, literacy research indicates that children's exposure to narrative texts varies significantly by economic and cultural status (e.g., Heath, 1982). Experiences with expository texts are even more limited in many households because they are not naturally associated with reading for leisure.

Most important, remember that graphic organizers are instructional tools, not worksheets. Instruction is needed. Regardless of the type of graphic organizer used, students, particularly those with LD and ELLs, need explicit instruction in how concepts are related (Dexter & Hughes, 2011). Problems that students with LD have with processing auditory language often result in short-term memory deficits and difficulty in understanding linguistic relationships. These students have particular difficulty organizing and categorizing information and need explicit instruction in how to make connections between and among concepts (Mercer & Mercer, 2005).

Table 6.3. Examples of text structure signal words

Cause/effect	Compare/contrast	Definition/example	Problem/solution	Proposition/support (temporal)
Because	However	For example	Because	For example
Consequently	But	For instance	Since	Therefore
If so, then	On the other hand	Specifically	Consequently	First, second, third
Since	Instead of	In addition	So that	Before
Therefore	As well as	Described as	Nevertheless	After
So that	Similar to	To illustrate	A solution	Then
Thus	Different from	Another	However	Finally
As a result	Compared to	First, second, third	Therefore	In conclusion
Not only, but			In addition	
			As a result	

From Sejnost, R.L., & Thiese, S.M. (2010). *Building content literacy*. Thousand Oaks, CA: Corwin Press; Republished by permission of Corwin Press, permission conveyed through Copyright Clearance Center, Inc.

 Caution 2

Teaching students *signal words* to help them identify text structure is a common teaching practice. Table 6.3 illustrates common signal words associated with each of the expository text structures. Teachers should use caution, however, when teaching signal words because they can be confusing or misleading for students in some texts. For example, notice that some words appear for multiple types of text structures—such as *however, first, therefore,* and *because.*

In addition, sometimes words on a signal words list are used in text but not as signal words for the text structure. A review of social studies textbooks suggested that signal words are found throughout textbooks, but often are not helpful for correctly identifying text structure (Berkeley et al., 2009). In fact, analysis of the texts showed that signal words were not helpful for identifying text structure 43% of the time. It is important for teachers to preview the text before teaching students to look for signal words to ensure that the writing lends itself to this type of approach. Furthermore, "it is important that students learn to focus on what the author is trying to communicate about the information in text rather than relying only on signal words" (Denton et al., 2012, p. 98).

WHAT ELSE DO TEACHERS NEED TO KNOW ABOUT TEXT STRUCTURE?

Considering the nature of narrative and expository texts, it is not completely surprising that research has shown that expository texts are more difficult for readers to recall and comprehend than narrative texts (e.g., Saenz & Fuchs, 2002). Expository texts are more challenging than narrative texts due to factors such as varied text structure, conceptual density, a large number of unfamiliar vocabulary terms, and insufficient prior knowledge (Englert &

Thomas, 1987; Taylor & Williams, 1983; Wong, 1980). Expository texts are especially challenging for students with LD who often lack strategies to help with reading comprehension, have limited vocabulary and/or prior knowledge of concepts, and do not have basic reading skills to gain access to text in which complex decoding skills are needed (Jitendra et al., 2001). In addition, ELLs may not be familiar with the text structures and organization of many U.S. textbooks and trade books.

Teachers often assess student understanding of information read through written products, such as summaries or reports, based on the assigned reading. Although the focus of this book is reading rather than writing, it is important that teachers should be careful not to assume that students can translate notes in a graphic organizer into a written product. Many students struggle to translate information represented in a graphic organizer into sentence and paragraph form. Therefore, it is important for teachers to remember that explicit instruction is needed here as well.

7

Teach Students to Read Strategically and Monitor Their Comprehension

Comprehension monitoring is a student's awareness of his or her understanding of what they read. This awareness can prompt the student to deal with problems in understanding as they arise, such as utilizing reading comprehension strategies. Students who cannot, or who do not, monitor their reading comprehension are likely to struggle more and learn less. Therefore, it is extremely important that teachers explicitly teach students to approach text in the strategic ways that good readers do.

WHAT IS STRATEGY INSTRUCTION AND WHY IS IT IMPORTANT FOR READING COMPREHENSION?

Students who struggle with reading do not strategically approach reading in the same way as good readers (see Chapter 1; Jones, Palincsar, Ogle, & Carr, 1987). However, a large body of research has found that students can be taught to approach text more like good readers through instruction in reading comprehension strategies (Edmonds et al., 2009; Gersten et al., 2001). Teaching students to use reading comprehension strategies looks very much like good instruction in general. The following practices are identified consistently as being important components of good instruction (Mastropieri et al., 2003; Swanson, 1999; Vaughn et al., 2000):

- Modeling
- Guided practice
- Independent practice
- Corrective feedback

A description of each of these instructional features follows.

Modeling

The purpose of modeling is to help students to conceptualize and apply new skills and strategies (Methe & Hintze, 2003; Rupley, Blair, & Nichols, 2009). Modeling of strategies often employs a *think-aloud*. Think-aloud is a teaching technique used to model cognitive processing for students by saying thoughts aloud during a problem-solving process (Block & Israel, 2004). This makes visible the thinking process that inherently is internal (Farr & Conner, 2004). The ultimate goal is that students will become strategic learners themselves and will "self-talk" their own cognitive processes as a means to regulate their own attention, strategy implementation, self-control, and reinforcement (Harris, Graham, Mason, & Friedlander, 2008).

In addition to modeling all of the strategy steps, it is important for teachers to model when and why a strategy should be used, how to be flexible in strategy selection and application, and how to make positive self-statements about progress, such as "*I did a good job summarizing the passage. I used all of the steps in the strategy and I tried hard. I will keep up the good work.*" (Berkeley, Mastropieri, & Scruggs, 2011; Regan & Berkeley, 2012). An example of using a think-aloud is provided later in the chapter in the modeling lesson for the QRAC-the-Code reading comprehension strategy (see also Chapter 5).

Guided and Independent Practice

It is important to provide guided practice opportunities after providing sufficient modeling of all of the strategy steps. The purpose of this practice is to guide students as they take increasing responsibility for task completion (Mercer & Mercer, 2005). When students eventually master the strategy steps, students will then practice using the strategy independently. It is important to provide opportunities for students to practice using self-regulation procedures that will help them apply reading comprehension strategies (Mastropieri & Scruggs, 2010). For more on self-regulation, see Text Box 7.1.

Corrective Feedback

Feedback is important for students' learning as well—specifically, feedback that helps students make connections between effort and performance. Targeted feedback can help students make connections between effort and success, which, in turn, enhances motivation, self-efficacy, and skills. Feedback can also help students make connections between insufficient effort and failure, which, in turn, promotes effort attributions and persistence (Schunk & Cox, 1986). For students who struggle with reading, beliefs about academic success and failure are thought to play a major role in determining motivation to learn and use cognitive and metacognitive strategies (see Chapter 8; Shell, Colvin, & Bruning, 1995).

Feedback is also important for students with disabilities who often do not persist in using strategies after instruction (Gersten et al., 2001; Vaughn

Text Box

7.1

DIG DEEPER

Self-Regulation

Self-regulation is a process that an individual employs to monitor and control behavior, including learning. Self-regulation is an important element of social cognitive theory (see Bandura, 1986) and involves setting goals, using strategies, managing time efficiently, monitoring behavior, evaluating progress, and reflecting on outcomes (Zimmerman, 2002). Many students develop effective strategies to help self-regulate academic demands of the secondary grades, but a significant number do not (Zimmerman & Martinez-Pons, 1990). Students with attention-deficit/hyperactivity disorder and learning disabilities (LD) especially struggle with self-regulation of behavior and learning. Zimmerman described self-regulation as having three primary phases: 1) forethought phase, 2) performance phase, and 3) self-reflection phase.

The *forethought phase* includes task analysis, which leads to goal setting and strategic planning to reach the goal. In the context of reading, this might translate to a *goal* to understand the assigned reading (or specific aspects of the content) and the selection of appropriate strategies that match the demands of the text and the skill level of the reader. This phase also includes self-motivational beliefs (self-efficacy, outcome expectations, intrinsic interest/value, and goal orientation).

The *performance phase* includes self-control (self-instruction, imagery, attention-focusing and task strategies) and self-observation (self-recording and self-experimentation). *Self-instruction* refers to the subverbalizations that the learner employs to "walk through the steps" of the task. In the context of reading, this would be focused toward the steps of the selected reading comprehension strategy. *Imagery* refers to the making of mental pictures that can help with representation of ideas and recall of information, including information read. *Attention focusing* is one of the most challenging aspects of self-regulated learning for adolescents (Zimmerman & Bandura, 1994); however, the ability to focus one's attention and tune out distractions (both external and internal) is important for learning. *Task strategies* refer to strategies that help students remember and use the target strategy, including boiling strategy steps down to the most critical components or developing a mnemonic to assist in remembering the steps. For students with learning challenges, such as students with LD, teachers often assist in this process. *Self-recording* refers to the method for which individuals track their observations about their performance. This process can help students focus on the important elements needed for improvement, but it is important for *self-monitoring* to focus on positive learning rather than purely on negative aspects of performance (otherwise learning may be undermined). This process can also help a student *self-experiment* with changes to effort and actions to determine the impact on performance.

Finally, the *self-reflection phase* refers to self-judgment (self-evaluation and causal attribution) and self-reaction (self-satisfaction and adaptive/defensive reactions). *Self-judgment* refers to the evaluation of one's performance and what the individual attributes as the cause of that outcome. For example, in a reading context, a good reader would likely attribute success both to ability and effort (including use of strategies). (See Chapter 8 for more information on how causal attributions can impact learning.) The most helpful standards for self-evaluation are not perfect perfor-mance, but rather standards that are difficult, yet attainable. *Self-reaction* can be pos-itive—in which a student has a sense of satisfaction for reaching a goal and learning; constructive—in which a student adapts his or her approach when he or she does not reach his or her goal; or negative—in which a student develops defensive behaviors (e.g., learned helplessness, procrastination, task avoidance, disengagement, apathy). Self-reflection can affect a learner's intrinsic interest in the task and self-efficacy beliefs about effort toward learning (Zimmerman & Kitsantas, 1999).

Research demonstrated that students can be taught these self-regulatory pro-cesses. For this reason, you will notice self-regulation aspects included in reading com-prehension strategy instruction.

---

et al., 2000). What does targeted feedback look like? If the point of feedback is to promote independent strategy use, then the teacher might say, "Nice job! You worked hard and followed all of the steps to the strategy!" If the student could not produce a correct answer, then the teacher might say, "What other strategies do you think could help you to find the answer?" By providing this type of feedback, the use of the strategy is reinforced. In addition, it shifts the ownership of the knowledge to the student (rather than viewing the teacher as the holder of the *right* answer).

Metacognition and Strategy Awareness

Strategy instruction includes more than just teaching students the steps in the strategy. For students to get the most out of strategy use, they also need to develop their metacognition—their knowledge and awareness of their think-ing, use of strategies to achieve goals, and monitoring of progress toward these goals (Lajoie, 2008). Within the context of reading, comprehension strategy awareness refers to a person's knowledge about specific task demands, includ-ing how to determine whether a strategy would be appropriate in addition to how to use the strategy itself (Pressley & Ghatala, 1990). This awareness is needed so that students are able to match appropriate strategies to a specific reading context. This may seem like something that students would pick up naturally, but the successful selection, application, and monitoring of strate-gies is extremely challenging for some students, such as those with learning disabilities (LD; Wixson & Lipson, 1991). Students who are metacognitively aware, however, tend to be more strategic in how they approach learning tasks and, as a result, tend to perform better (Deshler et al., 1996; Garner & Alexander, 1989; Pressley & Ghatala, 1990).

Metacognitive strategies focus on how students select, monitor, and use strategies (Lenz, Ellis, & Scanlon, 1996). Following are several areas that are important to address through explicit instruction in order to promote metacognition:

- Teach students *why* to use reading comprehension strategies.

- Teach students *how* to use comprehension strategies.

- Teach students *when* to use comprehension strategies.

- Teach students to *self-regulate* their use of comprehension strategies.

Students can be taught any number of strategies to facilitate the learning process, but strategies are only beneficial when students are motivated to maintain their use after instruction. One way to accomplish this is to help them learn to monitor their comprehension. If they are aware that they have not understood what they have read, then they are more likely to employ strategies to help themselves.

WHY IS COMPREHENSION MONITORING IMPORTANT FOR READING COMPREHENSION?

The process that readers use to monitor their own understanding of text is referred to as *comprehension monitoring* (National Reading Panel, 2000). Comprehension monitoring is something that good readers do while they are reading so that they are aware when they have not understood something. These students generally employ reading comprehension strategies to help *fix up* their understanding (Roberts, Torgesen, Boardman, & Scammacca, 2008). For example, if a reader is having difficulty understanding what is being read, then he or she may use knowledge of affixes and root words to help determine meanings of unknown words, use a graphic organizer to represent important ideas in the text, or try to identify the main idea of what was read. Struggling readers, however, often are unaware of when comprehension has broken down and as a result do not go back to repair problems with their understanding (Gersten et al., 2001; Roberts et al., 2008). It is important to explicitly teach students this critical skill.

WHAT DOES THIS LOOK LIKE IN INSTRUCTION?

Figure 7.1 is a modeling lesson of a self-questioning strategy that is used to help students monitor their comprehension while reading. The left-hand column contains a scripted excerpt from the teaching lesson that begins with modeling, then transitions to guided practice, and eventually to independent student practice in which the teacher monitors student proficiency and provides explicit strategy feedback. The right-hand column notes the critical components of the lesson. It should be noted, however, that the principles illustrated here can be applied to other reading strategies as well.

Excerpt from teaching	Characteristic
SAY: We know that good readers ask and answer questions in their head while they are reading. Today I am going to teach you a way to come up with good questions when you read your textbook.	The teacher sets a purpose for learning the strategy.
SAY: Let's look at the steps. Look at the strategy sheet in front of you and let's read it together:	The teacher provides students with a checklist of strategy steps.
"Understand Your Textbook: Be a DUCKtective and QRAC the Code!" **Q**uestion (Turn headings into questions) **R**ead (Read the section and STOP) **A**nswer (Ask yourself, "Can I answer my question?") **C**heck (Check to be sure your answer was correct OR summarize the section)	The teacher introduces each step of the strategy using a mnemonic to help students remember the steps.
SAY: Let's try it out! Turn to the first page in your packet. The title of this section is "The Scientific Revolution," so this is what everything we read today will be about. The first heading is "The Birth of Modern Science." The first thing that I need to do is turn the heading into *question*. Because I know this whole section is about the scientific revolution, my question will be, "Why was the scientific revolution called the birth of modern science?" That is already written down for me as the first example.	The teacher models the first step of the strategy using think-aloud.
SAY: The next step is *read*. So I need to read the section [read the section out loud].	The teacher models the second step of the strategy using think-aloud.
SAY: Okay, I read the section. Now I need to decide if I can *answer* my question. I think I can, so I will circle "yes"—that is done for me on the example too.	The teacher models the third step of the strategy using think-aloud.
SAY: The last step is to *check* that my answer is correct. I circled "yes" because I think that the scientific revolution is called the birth of modern science because it made people understand the world in a new way. This part said that before the scientific revolution, people relied on authorities such as Greek thinkers and the church to explain the world, but after the scientific revolution (was "born"), they relied on logic to explain what they saw in the world. So I think I was right.	The teacher models the fourth and final step of the strategy using think-aloud.

Heading	Question (answer)	Key concepts/check
The Birth of Modern Science	*Model:* Why was it called the birth of modern science? (Yes)	*Model:* Before the scientific revolution, people explained things based on what ancient writers or the Catholic Church said, but after modern science was "born," people explained things based on science

Figure 7.1. Modeling comprehension monitoring strategy: QRAC-the-Code. (*Source:* Berkeley & Riccomini, 2013.)

Excerpt from teaching	Characteristic
SAY: Okay. Now I will make questions for *all* of the other headings in the section titled "The Birth of Modern Science." 1. Read each heading. 2. Ponder turning it into a question. 3. Write the questions on the overhead. 4. Read one section. 5. Circle "yes" or "no" on the overhead (see table and scripts below). 6. Check that your answer was correct. Try a fix-up strategy (summarize if all else fails). 7. Repeat steps 4–6 until all answered questions are checked.	The teacher models multiple examples of each step of the strategy including nonexamples and additional positive examples using the same instructional sequence and modeling self-feedback for correctly following steps of the strategy each time.

Heading	Question (answer)	Key concepts/check
Understanding Science	Model: Who understands science? (No)* see script below	Model: Summary: Science is a way to understand the world through observations, experiments, and theories.

	Nonexamples help promote flexible strategy use by students.
*SAY: I am not sure about this one, so I will need to circle "no." Let's see if I can find some other clues. Look at the strategy sheet again. • Did you understand the <u>vocabulary</u>? *Look for the definition of bold words.* • Were there clues in the <u>text features</u>? *Study maps and graphs.* • Do you know anything else about the topic? *Use your prior knowledge.* • Was your question not answered? *Try to summarize the section instead.* ° Who was the section about? ° What happened in the section? ° Tell what the section was about in less than 2 sentences. • Really, really stuck? *Reread the section and try again.*	The teacher provides explicit modeling in how to problem solve alternate steps to take (and explicitly references the students' strategy steps sheet).
SAY: Those are all really good ideas for finding more clues. Let's see, this time I understood the vocabulary, so that might not help. And there were not any text features such as maps or graphs. Maybe this was not such a good question. I think I will summarize the section instead. • The section is about science. • Nothing really happens in the section, but it describes how science works, so this is what I will summarize in two sentences: • Science is a way to understand the world through observation, facts, logical ideas, and theories. Scientists use experiments to test whether their theories are correct.	The teacher models the implementation of these "fix-up" steps using think-aloud.
SAY: Good! Now I am positive that I understood the section, so I will move on to the next section: "Roots of the Revolution."	The teacher models giving self-praise.

WHAT IS THE BOTTOM LINE WITH STRATEGY INSTRUCTION?

This book has presented many instructional approaches that can assist students with comprehension. The ultimate goal, however, is for students to become independent learners. Reading strategies are *tools* that guide a student's access to text when support from the teacher is no longer present. Therefore, a goal of instruction should focus on preparing students to use strategies flexibly and independently. Although strong teacher modeling is fundamental so that students internalize the purpose for strategy use as well as learn any necessary steps, students should also be given ample opportunities to apply them independently. After all, they will not always have their teacher close by when they face challenging text and need to independently choose among a repertoire of strategies in order to make sense of what they read.

"Give a man a fish and you feed him for a day.
Teach a man to fish and you feed him for a lifetime."

Proverb

8

Motivation and the Struggling Reader

Although reading skills are certainly important, it is also important to consider and address issues of motivation and engagement. Many older students who have struggled in reading throughout their schooling lack motivation to persist on difficult tasks and become disinterested in reading. It is important for teachers to be aware of this and to take steps that help to reengage students in the reading process.

Good readers generally are motivated readers. Students who are poor readers, however, read too little, rarely read for deep understanding, seldom read to expand their sense of self or identities, and have more negative self-concepts of who they are as readers (e.g., Chapman, Tunmer, & Prochnow, 2000). Therefore, we cannot only focus on the cognitive dimensions of reading, but we also need to monitor how students think of themselves as readers. Why do they think that they succeed or fail when attempting to read and understand? We also need to explicitly address motivation and engagement as both are tightly connected to reading success.

HOW DO STUDENTS RESPOND TO PAST FAILURES IN READING?

When students experience repeated failures, it generally results in low perceptions of ability, negative academic self-concept, tendencies toward learned helplessness, and lower expectations for future school success (Borkowski, Carr, Rellinger, & Pressley, 1990; Chapman, 1988; Elliott & Dweck, 1988; Paris & Winograd, 1990). In addition, repeated failures contribute to students' beliefs that they have little control over their academic achievement (Dweck & Reppucci, 1973; Licht, Kistener, Ozkaragoz, Shapiro, & Clausen, 1985). As a result, these students often display low motivation and a passive approach to learning (Smey-Richman, 1991). Students who have consistent failing experiences look at failure and success quite differently than their proficient counterparts. For example, students who have a history of academic failure often believe that they have little control over their academic achievement or they make faulty conclusions about why they succeed or fail in school (Nelson & Manset-Williamson, 2006; Stipek, 1993; Stipek & Weiz, 1981). For example, students might believe that they do well only when tasks are easy or because they were lucky. Conversely, they may believe that they failed because someone else did not help them or because they are not smart enough. These beliefs about reasons for success and failure are called *causal attributions* (see Text Box 8.1).

Faulty attributional beliefs decrease the likelihood that these students will put forth the required effort to use reading strategies, particularly older students with learning disabilities (LD). For example, students with LD often attribute failure to lack of ability rather than inconsistent effort. Students with LD also are more likely to attribute successes to external causes (e.g., task difficulty) and failures to internal causes (e.g., ability or effort) than their typically developing peers (Borkowski, Weyhing, & Carr, 1988; Tabassam & Grainger, 2002). If effort is not valued as a cause for school success, then a student is unlikely to persist on academic tasks, particularly if the task is perceived to be challenging. This is a big problem when we consider that researchers have suggested that task persistence may be at least as important as knowledge of strategies in whether students successfully understand complex expository text (Gersten et al., 2001). Furthermore, inappropriate attributions of students with LD are often engrained due to experiencing years of failure in academic tasks. There is some beginning evidence, however, that positive attributions regarding effort can motivate students to acquire and persist in using strategies (Berkeley et al., 2011; Borkowski et al., 1988). Part of this involves helping students have more accurate perceptions of their own abilities.

"Our greatest weakness lies in giving up. The most certain way to succeed is always to try just one more time."

Thomas Edison, American inventor

Students' beliefs about their own abilities are referred to as *self-efficacy* (see Text Box 8.2). Reading self-efficacy consists of students' perceptions of their reading capabilities.

Text Box

8.1

DIG DEEPER

Causal Attribution Theory

The importance of attributions is incorporated from Causal Attribution Theory of Motivation and Emotions (e.g., Weiner, 1974, 1980, 1986), which maintains that "causal attributions can have a direct and important influence on a person's goals, emotions, and personal agency beliefs" (Ford, 1992, p. 164). In achievement contexts, students often attribute their successes and failures to ability, effort, task difficulty, and luck (Weiner, 1979). Research has shown that feedback that helps students make connections between effort and success enhances motivation, self-efficacy, and skills (Schunk, 1985; Schunk & Cox, 1986).

Causal attributions can be defined as one's judgments about the cause of success or failure in achievement situations (Shell et al., 1995; Weiner, 1985). Causal attribution beliefs are developmental processes (e.g., Bandura, 1986; Hiebert, Winograd, & Danner, 1984; Schunk, 1991), which is why young children commonly 1) have inaccurate perceptions of causality, 2) overestimate the contingency between their behaviors and outcomes, and 3) overstate their ability. However, most children's accuracy regarding ability beliefs increases with age and becomes more highly related to achievement (Paris & Oka, 1986; Stipek, 1993). There are some important exceptions that have particular relevance when considering older students who struggle with reading.

Young children tend to attribute success to both effort and ability. Older students, however, tend to believe that if they put in little effort, then they have high ability, and if they need to put in much effort, then they have low ability (Bandura, 1986; Dweck & Leggett, 1988; Shell et al., 1995; Weiner, 1985). As a result, older children tend to attribute success to effort less than younger children (Stipek, 1993). Furthermore, the influence of social comparisons may have a larger impact on learning with older students because unlike younger students, older students do not perceive success on easy tasks as an indicator of high ability (Stipek & Tannatt, 1984). Instead, students consider many factors, but particularly how well they are performing in comparison with classmates (Bear, Minke, Griffin, & Deemer, 1998). Finally, older students are likely to attempt challenging tasks only if they believe it is something that they are already good at (Bear et al., 1998; Morrone & Pintrich, 2006).

Finally, there are differences between high achievers and low achievers. Students who are efficacious are more likely to work hard, persist, and seek help so they can complete a task and, as a result, these students tend to be high achievers (Linnenbrink & Pintrich, 2003). Furthermore, compared to low achievers, high achievers tend to attribute causality for success more to internal causes (e.g., ability, effort) rather than external causes (e.g., luck, task difficulty, receiving assistance), and they have higher expectations for positive outcomes (Shell et al., 1995). It is not surprising then that these same students are more likely to use cognitive and metacognitive strategies to increase their understanding of what they read (Walker, 2003).

Text Box

8.2

DIG DEEPER

Self-Efficacy

It is well known that individuals are likely to persist and put more effort in those activities in which they believe they will be able to succeed. *Self-efficacy* is defined as an individual's beliefs in his or her capabilities to organize and execute the courses of action needed to succeed in specific tasks or situations (Bandura, 1977). Students' beliefs in their abilities to succeed in particular academic situations or tasks are important for several reasons. Self-efficacy beliefs can be a powerful predictor of achievement, such as measures of cognitive ability (Pajares & Kranzler, 1995) and reading achievement/ comprehension (e.g., Guthrie et al., 2004; Taboada Barber et al., in press). Understanding task demands is essential for developing self-efficacy beliefs and academic performance because they require consideration of the skills one possesses (Klassen, 2006).

Students with learning disabilities and English language learners do not always have a full grasp of the tasks at hand. This is especially true of literacy tasks when they are faced with multiple strategies to use without often knowing or understanding their purpose. Furthermore, they also struggle with various aspects of metacognition (Butler, 1998), which is the "thinking about thinking" that allows us to assess or evaluate the nature of the task at hand. Forming self-efficacy beliefs is a metacognitive process, requiring an awareness of the self and the task (Klassen, 2006). That is, in order to determine how good one is at a given task/activity, the latter needs to be fully understood first.

One of the important characteristics of successful individuals is that failure and adversity do not undermine their self-efficacy beliefs. This is because self-efficacy is not so much about learning how to succeed as it is about learning *how to persevere when one does not succeed*. Self-efficacy cannot provide the skills required to succeed, but it can provide the effort and persistence required to obtain those skills and use them effectively. (Pajares, 2006, p. 345)

Teachers can influence students' awareness of themselves as readers, as well as their efficacy beliefs. Given that students with LD sometimes struggle with metacognition (awareness of their own thinking and understanding), it is not surprising that these students tend to miscalibrate their self-efficacy beliefs (Klassen, 2006). In addition, teachers' anecdotal observations have indicated that English language learners (ELLs) often have low self-efficacy for reading and often a poor understanding of the purposes of many reading activities as they move through the upper elementary and middle grades. Researchers (e.g., Schunk & Miller, 2002) proposed several approaches that teachers can use to cultivate students' self-efficacy beliefs, including

- Help students set short-term goals that are achievable so they can work toward them in effective ways and become aware of their success when goals are met.

- Teach students *how* and *when* to use specific cognitive reading strategies.

- Provide opportunities to observe models completing the same or similar tasks so that students are exposed to the components of the task being performed.

- Teach students to recognize positive (self-promoting) and negative (self-defeating) thoughts and how to use positive self-talk.

- Provide specific feedback to teach students to attribute outcomes to strategic efforts. For example, instead of saying, "Good job," say, "Good job. I really liked how you tied your background knowledge to this section of text."

- Help students see where their strengths are and build on them by discussing them with individual students in relation to specific tasks.

WHY DOES MOTIVATION AND ENGAGEMENT MATTER FOR READING SUCCESS?

Abundant empirical research shows that reading for internal reasons such as enjoyment, desire to learn about favorite topics, and for sheer interest is conducive to reading achievement and increased comprehension. Reading engagement and reading achievement interact with each other in a spiral—high achievers read more, and the more they read, the more engaged they become and the higher they achieve. Lower achievers read less, and the less they read, the more disengaged they become with reading, and the lower they achieve (Guthrie, 2008).

Disengagement from reading has its roots in early years. For example, research has shown that first-grade students who struggle with reading see themselves as less competent readers and have more negative attitudes about reading than students who read at a high level (Morgan, Fuchs, Compton, Cordray, & Fuchs, 2008). Furthermore, teachers indicated that poor readers are less likely to read widely and frequently, read about favorite topics/activities, prefer reading during social settings, or write about what they read (Morgan et al., 2008). These early patterns of motivation and attitudes toward reading become entrenched as students move through the grades, such that by the time they transition in middle school, declines in academic motivation and performance are well established (e.g., Anderman, Maehr, & Midgley, 1999; Jacobs, Lanza, Osgood, Eccles, & Wigfield, 2002). In fact, many struggling readers are demotivated, apathetic, or resistant to reading. Furthermore, these students have little interest in reading for pleasure, and they report not believing they can read well enough to understand the books used daily in class. Their beliefs in their capacity to understand through reading are severely diminished. Therefore, in addition to teaching students skills and strategies in the area of reading, it is also important to address factors related to engagement and motivation.

Engagement versus Motivation

Engagement and *motivation* are related terms and are often used inter-changeably (e.g., National Research Council, 2004). However, the two should be differentiated. *Student engagement* refers to student involvement, participation, and commitment. Experts on student engagement describe it as a manifestation or an expression of motivated action. Engagement presupposes motivation. That is, when a child is engaged in a book or in a task, his or her emotions, attention, goals, and other psychological processes that are involved in motivation are present. *Engagement,* however, is more of an umbrella term that includes behavioral, emotional, and cognitive dimensions (e.g., Fredericks, Blumenfeld, & Paris, 2004).

Behavioral engagement at school has been described in the forms of listening carefully, showing effort and persisting with academic activities, and participating in class discussions (e.g., Fredericks et al., 2004). It has also been characterized as zest and enthusiasm for learning and academic tasks (e.g., Skinner, Kindermann, & Furrer, 2009). Because reading is inherently cognitive, some of the effort in behavioral engagement is cognitive. *Cognitive engagement* refers to intention and effort to be actively involved in the reading (e.g., by using cognitive strategies) as well as through the dedication, time investment, and commitment toward reading activities (Guthrie, Wigfield, & You, 2012).

Reading engagement, in particular, has been described as the fusion of cognitive and motivation processes that takes place as the student approaches and deals with the act of reading. Thus, students who are engaged readers are motivated to read by showing interest, involvement, attention, concentration, and perseverance, but they are cognitively invested in their reading as well. As such, they actively use cognitive strategies such as asking questions or monitoring their comprehension while reading.

Teachers are quite used to determining which students are more engaged or less engaged in their classrooms by simply observing student behaviors and actions. We are all familiar with the student whose head is down, the student whose eyes are blank or fixated somewhere else but the task at hand, or the student who initiates a task but loses focus quite soon. These students are likely to use superficial strategies, if any, while reading; easily lose track of content and key ideas; and become disinterested in reading right away. Teachers fortunately are also familiar with the opposite case—the insistent hands-up participant, the diligent task completer, and the avid reader who comes back with curious questions. Yet, we also are well aware of those students in between, those who straddle between being interested and easily losing it. These students put effort into their reading, but fail to persist if the task is too complex or the topic is too foreign or new.

Many people think that motivation is an ingrained, inherited trait, just like whether you have blue or brown eyes. You either have it or do not (or you have it for certain things and not for others). Although we are all more intrinsically motivated for some activities than others, school reading is not an option for students. Reading during school time is most likely the only opportunity to build knowledge and learn from reading for many students, especially those who live in poverty or struggle with reading. It is this school-based reading that can launch them to reading outside of school and for their own enjoyment.

HOW CAN TEACHERS ADDRESS
MOTIVATION AND ENGAGEMENT IN THE CLASSROOM?

Research repeatedly has shown that supports that teachers provide during classroom instruction are strongly related to outcomes of reading achievement, motivation, and engagement (Guthrie et al., 2012). How can teachers help with student motivation in the classroom? There are some research-based practices that have shown to increase student motivation for reading and students' reading engagement, both for English monolingual students (e.g., Guthrie et al., 2004; Guthrie, Mcrae, & Klauda, 2007) and for ELLs (Taboada & Rutherford, 2011; Taboada Barber et al., in press).

Knowledge Goals

One engagement-supporting practice is the use of knowledge goals in reading tasks. This practice has also been found to significantly improve reading comprehension (e.g., Guthrie et al., 2007). *Knowledge goals* simply refer to the organization of content units around themes that explain substantial principles of a domain (Cox & Guthrie, 2002). Teachers can easily draw from these to organize reading topics around thematic units because of the explicitness of content standards. The idea is to organize content around "a limited set of powerful ideas (basic understandings and principles)" (Brophy, 1999, p. 80). Students engage in deep processing of text and comprehend more when a knowledge goal is the driving question of instruction than when the emphasis is on trivial facts or performance goals (e.g., to do better than your classmates; Benware & Deci, 1984; Meece, Blumenfeld, & Hoyle, 1988; Taylor, Pearson, Clark, & Walpole, 2000). Furthermore, reading to build knowledge (and not merely to learn to apply strategies or vocabulary skills) imbues reading activities with a clear purpose that is in itself motivating.

Knowledge goals are best exemplified through conceptual themes (i.e., themes that are organized around central concepts within a unit or domain; see Chapter 2 for additional benefits to this approach for students working on basic reading skills). For example, a life science unit that is organized around the topic of "Adaptations to the Environment" can prompt reading about mammals' and birds' types of adaptations (or simply one species' adaptations) so that students are reading and learning about key concepts through different topics. Having students just read about different types of birds without a unifying theme would not be an example of a conceptual theme. Similarly, when first introducing the idea of chemistry for an introductory high school chemistry class, the teacher may choose to have students read articles and collect artifacts behind household items such as cosmetics, perfumes, medicine, household cleaners, soap, and toothpaste. The unifying theme would be to learn what is common and what is different about the chemical composition of these items. The broad concept of chemistry is at the center of all this reading and exploration. Knowledge goals for reading can be more easily set if subtopics or key concepts are preselected by teachers before embarking on a broad theme.

Abundance of Interesting Texts

An abundance of interesting texts for comprehension instruction is critical to fostering students' engagement in reading. Research indicates that students showed better comprehension of texts rated as more interesting than of texts rated as less interesting (Alexander, Jetton, & Kulikowich, 1995; Schiefele, 1999).

Abundant texts also have advantages over textbooks for some learning purposes. Limiting students to the exclusive use of the textbook seems rather coercive when the goal is to give students the opportunity to get involved and engaged in sustained reading. Textbooks tend to cover topics in abbreviated forms so as to meet the priorities of extensive curricula. Although textbooks are needed for essential content, students will be engaged in their reading and motivated to read if they get exposure and can read extensively about a topic. For example, students who are learning about Teddy Roosevelt's presidency might read books that span his presidency, his foreign policy legacy, his civic involvement, his role in fighting business monopolies, his early childhood health struggles, and his love of nature and his pivotal role in creating the national parks. The students benefit from the opportunity of developing expertise on a topic when time for extensive reading on a topic is prioritized. In addition, they have the opportunity to engage with the materials and the content in ways that are not feasible when piecemeal treatment of multiple topics and teaching to the test are exclusively emphasized.

Student Collaboration in Reading

Teacher support for student collaboration in reading activities is another important engagement-supporting practice. Several instructional programs (e.g., Guthrie et al., 2004; Scardamalia, Bereiter, & Lamon, 1994) have characterized social, knowledge-building contexts as important for reading comprehension, conceptual learning, and reading engagement, especially for students of diverse backgrounds (Au, 1998). Students themselves express positive influences for small-group interactions and discussions about texts. For instance, Juan, a sixth-grade ELL, said, "In a group it is easier. You have people to think with. What is the main idea? And that has got to be easier." Miguel, a fourth-grade student, expressed, "I like working with my buddies in small groups when we read; we get to talk about dangerous animals and how they are at the top of the food chain. If I am reading alone all the time, it is boring. I do not get to discuss this."

The important thing for teachers to bear in mind is that if social collaboration around literacy is to be productive and engaging, then the fun of small-group collaboration cannot be dominated by the prevalence of trivial talk. Students need well-structured, goal-driven literacy-related tasks in which they are all accountable for a common (group) goal and where individual responsibilities are clear for each team member. Teacher monitoring and scaffolding is essential for effective collaboration in reading to succeed.

Autonomy Support

Autonomy support consists of enabling students to control significant elements of their reading and writing (Guthrie, 2008). Feeling in control and self-directed in their reading is a powerful motivator, especially for struggling young adolescents. Autonomy support takes different forms. Two of the most investigated by educational psychologists are 1) fostering relevance by explaining the role of the learning activity in relation to the students' personal goals or everyday lives (i.e., Why is this important to learn today? How is this relevant to your learning and/or your life? How does this reading strategy help you with your reading?) and 2) providing students with meaningful academic choices. Teachers can do multiple things to establish relevance, from providing hands-on activities for science to taking students to a local museum so they can interact with primary documents and artifacts before learning a specific topic in history. Teachers clearly conveying and discussing the importance of why they are learning what they are learning are equally important for fostering relevance. Although this may not be possible for every aspect of a mandated curricula, multiple aspects of learning can be justified or explained to students. This is especially important for adolescents who tend to question almost every aspect, including the purpose of school. This can be accomplished by posing questions to students such as

- Why do we care about activating our knowledge about text? How does it help us?

- Why is it useful to ask questions during and after reading?

- How do summaries help with our reading?

- When do you think summarizing may become especially helpful to you?

- Why do good readers monitor their comprehension?

The impact of relevance-fostering statements/questions for student awareness of the usefulness of strategies and their bearing for current and future reading cannot be underestimated.

In relation to affording student choice, it is fundamental that these choices are perceived as meaningful by the students in addition to addressing the content to be learned. Choice of books to read within subthemes of a theme, choice of strategy to apply out of a menu of teacher preselected ones, and choice of media to present a unit final project are just a few. Many studies confirmed the value of autonomy support in instruction (e.g., Perencevich, 2004; Stefanou, Perencevich, DiCintio, & Turner, 2004). Students show increased reading activity and comprehension when they perceive that instruction is relevant to their lives (Lau, 2009; Reynolds & Symons, 2001).

FINAL THOUGHTS

Many students struggle to understand what they read either due to basic reading difficulties that hinder their access to the text or a failure to strategically approach text. These students include both students with LD and ELLs. Teaching these students how to better understand text includes employing an array of instructional approaches before, during, and after reading. It also includes teaching students strategies that they can independently use when reading.

> Competency in reading is necessary but insufficient by itself to engender better academic performance. Students need to be self-regulating not only to become more successful academically, but also to be able to employ their skills flexibly long after they leave school. (Biancarosa & Snow, 2004, p.16)

Teachers can help students gain meaning from text with support and independently. They can also make instructional decisions that help to motivate and reengage struggling readers. These efforts can make all the difference for these students.

References

Adler, C.R. (2001). *Seven strategies to teach students text comprehension.* Retrieved from http://readingrockets.org

Alexander, P.A., Jetton, T.L., & Kulikowich, J.M. (1995). Interrelationship of knowledge, interest, and recall: Assessing a model of domain learning. *Journal of Educational Psychology, 87,* 559–575. doi:10.1037/0022-0663.87.4.559

Allen, J. (1999). *Words, words, words: Teaching vocabulary in grades 4–12.* Portland, ME: Stenhouse Publishers.

Alverman, D.E., Phelps, S.F., & Gillis, V.R. (2010). *Content area reading and literacy: Succeeding in today's diverse classrooms.* Boston, MA: Allyn & Bacon.

American Speech-Language-Hearing Association. (2005). *Helping children with communication disorders in the schools.* Retrieved from http://www.readingrockets.org

American Speech-Language-Hearing Association. (2013). *Social language use: Pragmatics.* Retrieved from http://www.asha.org/public/speech/development/pragmatics.htm

Anderman, E.M., Maehr, M.L., & Midgley, C. (1999). Declining motivation after the transition to middle school: Schools can make a difference. *Journal of Research & Development in Education, 32,* 131–147.

Anderson, R.C. (1984). Role of the reader's schema in comprehension, learning, and memory. In R.C. Anderson, J. Osborn, & R.J. Tierney (Eds.), *Learning to read in American schools: Basal readers and content texts* (pp. 243–258). Mahwah, NJ: Lawrence Erlbaum Associates.

Anderson, R.C., & Nagy, W.E. (1991). Word meanings. In R. Barr, M.L. Kamil, P. Mosenthal, & P.D. Pearson (Eds.), *Handbook of Reading Research* (Vol. II, pp. 690–724). New York, NY: Longman.

Anderson, R.C., Wilson, P.T., & Fielding, L.G. (1988). Growth in reading and how children spend their time outside of school. *Reading Research Quarterly, 23,* 285–303.

Anglin, J.M. (1993). Vocabulary development: A morphological analysis. *Monographs of the Society for Research in Child Development, 58*(10), 1–186.

Anonymous (March 21, 2005). Armed and dangerous: Robot soldiers. *Junior Scholastic, 107*(15), 3.

Armbruster, B., & Nagy, W.E. (1992). Vocabulary in content area lessons. *The Reading Teacher, 7,* 550–551.

Au, K.H. (1998). Social constructivism and the school literacy learning of students of diverse backgrounds. *Journal of Literacy Research, 30,* 297–319. doi:10.1080/10862969809548000

August, D., & Shanahan, T. (Eds.). (2006). *Developing literacy in second-language learners: Report of the National Literacy Panel on language-minority children and youth.* Mahwah, NJ: Lawrence Erlbaum Associates.

Baker, S.K., Simmons, D.C., & Kame'enui, E.J. (1998). Vocabulary acquisition: Instruction and curricular basics and implications. In D.C. Simmons & E.J. Kame'enui (Eds.), *What reading research tells us about children with diverse learning needs: Bases and basics* (pp. 219–238). Mahwah, NJ: Lawrence Erlbaum Associates.

Bandura, A. (1977). *Social learning theory.* Upper Saddle River, NJ: Prentice Hall.

Bandura, A. (1986). *Social foundations of thought and action: A social cognitive theory.* Upper Saddle River, NJ: Prentice Hall.

Barone, M.D., & Xu, S.H. (2008). *Literacy instruction for English language learners: PreK–6.* New York, NY: Guilford Press.

Baumann, J.F., & Bergeron, B.S. (1993). Story map instruction using children's literature: Effects on first graders' comprehension of central narrative elements. *Journal of Literacy Research, 25,* 407–437. doi:10.1080/10862969309547828

Baumann, J.F., Kame'enui, E.J., & Ash, G. (2003). Research on vocabulary instruction: Voltaire redux. In J. Flooe, D. Lapp, J.R. Squire, & J. Jensen (Eds.), *Handbook of research on teaching the English language arts* (2nd ed., pp. 752–785). Mahwah, NJ: Lawrence Erlbaum Associates.

Baumert, J., Nagy, G., & Lehmann, R. (2012). Cumulative advantages and the emergence of social and ethnic inequality: Matthew effects in reading and mathematics development within elementary schools? *Child Development, 83,* 1347–1367.

Bear, D.R., Invernizzi, M., Templeton, S., & Johnston, F. (2000). *Words their way: Word study for phonics, vocabulary, and spelling instruction* (2nd ed.). Upper Saddle River, NJ: Prentice Hall.

Bear, G.G., Minke, K.M., Griffin, S.M., & Deemer, S.A. (1998). Achievement-related perceptions of children with learning disabilities and normal achievement: Group and developmental differences. *Journal of Learning Disabilities, 31,* 91–104.

Beck, I.L., McKeown, M.G., & Kucan, L. (2013). *Bringing words to life: Robust vocabulary instruction.* New York, NY: Guilford Press.

Beck, I.L., McKeown, M.G., & Omanson, R.C. (1987). The effects and uses of diverse instructional techniques. In M.G. McKeown & M.E. Curtis (Eds.), *The nature of vocabulary acquisition* (pp. 147–163). Mahwah, NJ: Lawrence Erlbaum Associates.

Beech, J.R., & Keys, A. (1997). Reading vocabulary and language preference in 7-to 8-year-old bilingual Asian children. *Educational Psychology, 67,* 405–414. doi: 10.1111/j.2044-8279.1997.tb01254.x

Benware, C.A., & Deci, E.L. (1984). Quality of learning with an active versus passive motivational set. *American Educational Research Journal, 21,* 755–765. doi:10.3102/00028312021004755

Berkeley, S., Bender, W.N., Peaster, L.G., & Saunders, L. (2009). Implementation of response to intervention: A snapshot of progress. *Journal of Learning Disabilities, 42,* 85–95. doi:10.1177/0022219408326214

Berkeley, S., King-Sears, M.E., Hott, B.L., & Bradley-Black, K. (2014). Are history textbooks more "considerate" after 20 years? *Journal of Special Education, 47,* 217–230.

Berkeley, S., King-Sears, M., Vilbas, J., & Conklin, S. (2012, April). *Textbook characteristics that support or thwart comprehension: An evaluation of social studies texts.* Paper presented at the annual meeting of the American Education Research Association, Vancouver, British Columbia, Canada.

Berkeley, S., & Lindstrom, J.H. (2011). Technology for the struggling reader: Free and easily accessible resources. *Teaching Exceptional Children, 43,* 48–55.

Berkeley, S., Mastropieri, M.A., & Scruggs, T.E. (2011). Reading comprehension strategy instruction and attribution retraining for secondary students with learning and other mild disabilities. *Journal of Learning Disabilities, 44,* 18–32.

Berkeley, S., & Riccomini, P.J. (2013). QRAC-the-Code: A comprehension monitoring strategy for middle school social studies textbooks. *Journal of Learning Disabilities, 46,* 154–165.

Berkeley, S., & Scruggs, T.E. (2010). Current practice alerts: A focus on vocabulary instruction. *Division for Learning Disabilities (DLD) and Division for Research (DR) of the Council for Exceptional Children, Issue 18.*

Berkeley, S., Scruggs, T.E., & Mastropieri, M.A. (2010). Reading comprehension instruction for students with learning disabilities, 1995–2006: A meta-analysis. *Remedial and Special Education, 31,* 423–436.

Biancarosa, C., & Snow, C.E. (2004). *Reading next—A vision for action and research in middle school and high school literacy; A report to Carnegie Corporation of New York* (2nd ed.). Washington, DC: Alliance for Excellent Education.

Biancarosa, G. (2012). Adolescent literacy: More than remediation. *Educational Leadership, 69*(6), 22–27.

Blachman, B.A., Schatschneider, C., Fletcher, J.M., Francis, D.J., Clonan, S.M., Shaywitz, B.A., & Shaywitz, S.E. (2004). Effects of intensive reading remediation for second and third graders and a 1 year follow-up. *Journal of Educational Psychology, 96,* 444–461.

Block, C.C., & Israel, S.E. (2004). The ABC's of performing highly effective think-alouds. *The Reading Teacher, 58,* 154–167.

Borkowski, J.G., Carr, M., Rellinger, L., & Pressley, M. (1990). Self-regulated cognition: Inter-dependence of metacognition, attributions and self-esteem. In B.J. Jones, & L. Idol (Eds.), *Dimensions of thinking and cognitive instruction* (pp. 53–92). Mahwah, NJ: Lawrence Erlbaum Associates.

Borkowski, J.G., Weyhing, R.S., & Carr, M. (1988). Effects of attributional retraining on strategy-based reading comprehension in learning disabled students. *Journal of Educational Psychology, 80,* 46–53.

Bouffard, T., & Couture, N. (2003). Motivational profile and academic achievement among students enrolled in different schooling tracks. *Educational Studies, 29,* 19–38.

Boyle, J.R., & Weishaar, M. (1997). The effects of expert-generated versus student-generated cognitive organizers on the reading comprehension of students with learning disabilities. *Learning Disabilities Research and Practice, 12,* 228–235.

Brigham, F., & Brigham, M. (2001). Current practice alerts: A focus on mnemonic instruc-tion. *Division for Learning Disabilities (DLD) and Division for Research (DR) of the Council for Exceptional Children, Issue 5.*

Broer, N., Aarnoutse, C., Kieviet, F., & Van Leeuwe, J. (2002). The effects of instructing the structural aspects of text. *Educational Studies, 28,* 213–238.

Brophy, J. (1999). Toward a model of the value aspects of motivation in education: Developing appreciation for particular learning domains and activities. *Educational Psychologist, 34,* 75–85. doi:10.1207/s15326985ep3402_1

Bryant, D.P., Goodwin, M., Bryant, B.R., & Higgins, K. (2003). Vocabulary instruction for students with learning disabilities: A review of the research. *Learning Disability Quar-terly, 26,* 117–128.

Butler, D.L. (1998). Metacognition and learning disabilities. In B.Y.L. Wong (Ed.), *Learning about learning disabilities* (2nd ed., pp. 277–307). San Diego, CA: Academic Press.

Caldwell, J.S., & Leslie, L. (2005). *Intervention strategies to accompany informal reading assessment: So what do I do now?* Boston, MA: Allyn & Bacon.

Calkins, L. (2001). *The art of teaching reading.* New York, NY: Longman.

Carlisle, J.F. (2000). Awareness of the structure and meaning of morphologically complex words: Impact on reading. *Reading and Writing: An Interdisciplinary Journal, 12,* 169–190.

Carlisle, J.F., Beeman, M., Davis, L.H., & Spharim, G. (1999). Relationship of metalinguistic capabilities and reading achievement for children who are becoming bilingual. *Applied Psycholinguistics, 20,* 459–478. doi: 10.1017/S0142716499004014

Carlisle, J.F., & Rice, M.S. (2002). *Improving reading comprehension: Research-based principles and practices.* Baltimore, MD: York.

Carlo, M.S., August, D., McLaughlin, B., Snow, C.E., Dressler, C., Lippman, D.N., & White, C.E. (2004). Closing the gap: Addressing the vocabulary needs of English language learn-ers in bilingual and mainstream classrooms. *Reading Research Quarterly, 39,* 188–215.

Carnegie Council on Advancing Adolescent Literacy. (2010). *Time to act: An agenda for advancing adolescent literacy for college and career success.* New York, NY: Carnegie Corporation of New York.

Center, Y., Freeman, L., Robertson, G., & Outhred, L. (1999). The effect of visual imagery training on the reading and listening comprehension of low listening comprehenders in Year 2. *Journal of Research in Reading, 22,* 241–256. doi:10.1111/1467-9817.00088

Chall, J.S. (1983). *Stages of reading development.* New York, NY: McGraw-Hill.

Champagne, A.B., Gunstone, R.F., & Klopfer, L.E. (1985). Instructional consequences of stu-dents' knowledge about physical phenomena. In L.H.T. West & A.L. Pines (Eds.), *Cognitive structure and conceptual change* (pp. 61–91). Orlando, FL: Academic Press.

Chapman, J.W. (1988). Cognitive-motivational characteristics and academic achievement of learning disabled children: A longitudinal study. *Journal of Educational Psychology, 80,* 357–365.

Chapman, J.W., & Tunmer, W.E. (2003). Reading difficulties, reading-related self-perceptions, and strategies for overcoming negative self-beliefs. *Reading and Writing Quarterly, 19,* 5–24.

Chapman, J.W., Tunmer, W.E., & Prochnow, J.E. (2000). Early reading-related skills and perfor-mance, reading self-concept, and the development of academic self-concept: A longitudinal study. *Journal of Educational Psychology, 92,* 703–708. doi:10.1037/0022-0663.92.4.703

Chard, D.J., Vaughn, S., & Tyler, B.J. (2002). A synthesis of research on effective interventions for building reading fluency with elementary students with learning disabilities. *Journal of Learning Disabilities, 35,* 386–406.

Cole, J., & Degen, B. (1995). *The magic school bus: Inside a hurricane.* New York, NY: Scholastic.

Coleman, D., & Pimentel, S. (2012). *Revised publishers' criteria for the Common Core State Standards in English language arts and literacy: Grades 3–12.* Retrieved from http://www.corestandards.org/assets/Publishers_Criteria_for_3-12.pdf

Colorin Colorado. (2007). *Using cognates to develop comprehension in English.* Retrieved from http://www.colorincolorado.org/educators/background/cognates

Conner, J. (2004). *Using think alouds to improve reading comprehension.* Retrieved from http://www.readingrockets.org

Cortiella, C. (2008). *Study supports improved ways to identify learning disabilities.* Retrieved from http://www.ncld.org

Cox, K., & Guthrie, J.T. (2002). Concept instruction with text. In B. Guzzetti (Ed.), *Literacy in America: An encyclopedia of history, theory, and practice* (pp. 90–93). New York, NY: ABC-CLIO Publishers.

Cunningham, A.E., & Stanovich, K.E. (1998). What reading does for the mind. *American Educator, 22,* 8–15.

Dale, E. (1965). Vocabulary measurement: Technique and major findings. *Elementary English, 42,* 82–88.

Davis, L., Carlisle, J., & Beeman, M. (1999). Hispanic children's writing in English and Spanish when English is the language of instruction. *Yearbook of the National Reading Confer-ence, 48,* 238–248.

Denton, C.A., Vaughn, S., Wexler, J., Bryan, D., & Reed, D.S. (2012). *Effective instruction for middle school students with reading difficulties: The reading teacher's sourcebook.* Baltimore, MD: Paul H. Brookes Publishing Co.

Denton, C.A., Wexler, J., Vaughn, S., & Bryan, D. (2008). Intervention provided to linguisti-cally diverse middle school students with severe reading difficulties. *Learning Disabilities Research and Practice, 23,* 79–89.

Deshler, D.E., Ellis, E.S., & Lenz, B.K. (1996). *Teaching adolescents with learning disabil-ities* (2nd ed.). Denver, CO: Love Publishing.

Dexter, D.D., & Hughes, C.A. (2011). Graphic organizers and students with learning disabili-ties: A meta-analysis. *Learning Disability Quarterly, 34,* 51–72.

Dochy, F., Segers, M., & Buehl, M.M. (1999). The relation between assessment practices and outcomes of studies: The case of research on prior knowledge. *Review of Educational Research, 69,* 145–186.

Donovan, M.S., & Cross, C.T. (Eds.). (2002). *Minority students in special and gifted edu-cation.* Washington, DC: National Academies Press.

Dougherty Stahl, K.A., & Stahl, S.A. (2012). Young word wizards! Fostering vocabulary devel-opment in preschool and primary education. In E.J. Kame'enui & J.F. Baumann (Eds.), *Vocabulary instruction: Research to practice* (2nd ed., pp. 72–92). New York, NY: Guil-ford Press.

Duke, N.K., & Pearson, P.D. (2002). Effective practices for developing reading comprehension. In A.E. Farstrup & S.J. Samuels (Eds.), *What research has to say about reading instruc-tion* (3rd ed., pp. 205–242). Newark, DE: International Reading Association.

Durgunoglu, A.Y., Nagy, W.E., & Hancin-Bhatt, B.J. (1993). Cross-language transfer of pho-nological awareness. *Journal of Educational Psychology, 85,* 453-465. (Also reprinted in Consortium on Reading Excellence. (1999). *Reading research anthology: The why of reading instruction* (pp. 72–76). Novato, CA: Arena Press.)

Dweck, C.S., & Leggett, E.L. (1988). A social cognitive approach to motivation and personality. *Psychological Review, 95,* 256–273.

Dweck, C.S., & Reppucci, N.D. (1973). Learned helplessness and reinforcement responsibility in children. *Journal of Personality and Social Psychology, 25,* 109–116.

Dymock, S. (2007). Comprehension strategy instruction: Teaching narrative text structure awareness. *The Reading Teacher, 61,* 161–167. doi:10.1598/RT.61.2.6

Ebbers, S.M., & Denton, C.A. (2008). A root awakening: Vocabulary instruction for older students with reading difficulties. *Learning Disabilities Research and Practice, 23,* 90–102.

Edmonds, M.S., Vaughn, S., Wexler, J., Reutebuch, C., Cable, A., Tackett, K.K., & Schnakenberg, J.W. (2009). A synthesis of reading interventions and effects on reading comprehension outcomes for older struggling readers. *Review of Educational Research, 79,* 262–300.

Elliott, E.S., & Dweck, C.S. (1988). Goals: An approach to motivation and achievement. *Journal of Personality and Social Psychology, 54,* 5–12.

Ellis, E.S., & Howard, P.W. (2007). Graphic organizers: Power tools for teaching students with learning disabilities. *Division for Learning Disabilities (DLD) and Division for Research (DR) of the Council for Exceptional Children, Issue 13.*

Englert, C., & Mariage, T. (1991). Making students partners in the comprehension process: Organizing the reading "POSSE." *Learning Disability Quarterly, 14,* 123–138.

Englert, C.S., & Thomas, C.C. (1987). Sensitivity to text structure in reading and writing: A comparison between learning disabled and non-learning disabled students. *Learning Disability Quarterly, 10,* 93–105.

Farr, R., & Conner, J. (2004). *Using think-alouds to build reading comprehension.* Retrieved from http://www.ldonline.org

Feldman, K., & Kinsella, K. (2005). *Narrowing the language gap: The case of explicit vocabulary instruction.* New York, NY: Scholastic Professional Paper.

Fisher, D., & Frey, N. (2009). *Background knowledge: The missing piece of the comprehension puzzle.* Portsmouth, NH: Heinemann.

Fisher, D., Frey, N., & Lapp, D. (2008). Shared readings: Modeling comprehension, vocabulary, text structures, and text features for older readers. *The Reading Teacher, 61,* 548–556. doi:10.1598/RT.61.7.4

Foorman, B.R., Francis, D.J., Novy, D.M., & Liberman, D. (1991). How letter–sound instruction mediates progress in first-grade reading and spelling. *Journal of Educational Psychology, 83,* 456–469.

Ford, M.E. (1992). *Motivating humans: Goals, emotions, and personal agency beliefs.* Thousand Oaks, CA: Sage Publications.

Fountas, I.C. (2001). *Guiding readers and writers, grades 3-6: Teaching comprehension, genre, and content literacy.* Portsmouth, NH: Heinemann.

Fountas, I.C., & Pinnell, G.S. (2001). *Guiding readers and writers: Teaching comprehension, genre, and content literacy.* Portsmouth, NH: Heinemann.

Fox, B.J. (2010). *Phonics and structural analysis for the teacher of reading programmed for self-instruction.* Boston, MA: Allyn & Bacon.

Fredericks, J.A., Blumenfeld, P.C., & Paris, A.H. (2004). School engagement: Potential of the concept, state of the evidence. *Review of Educational Research, 74,* 59–109.

Fuchs, L.S., & Vaughn, S. (2012). Responsiveness-to-intervention: A decade later. *Journal of Learning Disabilities, 45,* 195–203.

Fulk, B.M., Brigham, F.J., & Lohman, D.A. (1998). Motivation and self-regulation: A comparison of students with learning and behavior problems. *Remedial and Special Education, 19,* 300–309.

Gajria, M., Jitendra, A.K., Sood, S., & Sacks, G. (2007). Improving comprehension of expository text in students with LD: A research synthesis. *Journal of Learning Disabilities, 40,* 210–225.

Gajria, M., & Salvia, J. (1992). The effects of summarization instruction on text comprehension of students with learning disabilities. *Exceptional Children, 58,* 508–516.

Ganske, K. (2010). Active thinking and engagement: Comprehension in the intermediate grades. In K. Ganske & D. Fisher (Eds.), *Comprehension across the curriculum: Perspectives and practices K–12* (pp. 96–118). New York, NY: Guilford Press.

Garcia, G.E. (1991). Factors influencing the English reading test performance of Spanish-speaking Hispanic children. *Reading Research Quarterly, 26,* 371–392.

Garner, R., & Alexander, P.A. (1989). Metacognition: Answered and unanswered questions. *Educational Psychologists, 24,* 143–158.

Genesee, F., & Geva, E. (2006). Cross-linguistic relationships in working memory, phonological processes, and oral language. In D. August & T. Shanahan (Eds.), *Report of the National Literacy Panel on K–12 youth and adolescents* (pp. 169–177). Mahwah, NJ: Lawrence Erlbaum Associates.

Genesee, F., & Riches, C. (2006). Instructional issues in literacy development. In F. Genesee, K. Lindholm-Leary, W. Saunders, & D. Christian (Eds.), *Educating English language learners: A synthesis of research evidence* (pp. 109–175). New York, NY: Cambridge University Press.

Gersten, R., Fuchs, L.S., Williams, J.P., & Baker, S. (2001). Teaching reading comprehension strategies to students with learning disabilities: A review of research. *Review of Educational Research, 71,* 279–320.

Geva, E., Yaghoub-Zadeh, Z., & Schuster, B. (2000). Understanding differences in word recognition skills of ESL children. *Annals of Dyslexia, 50,* 123–154.

Gillet, J.W., Temple, C., & Crawford, A.N. (2004). *Understanding reading problems: Assessment and instruction.* Boston, MA: Pearson.

Goldman, S.R., & Rakestraw, J.A. (2000). Structural aspects of constructing meaning from text. In R. Barr, M.L. Kamil, P. Mosenthal, & P.D. Pearson (Eds.), *Handbook of reading research* (Vol. III, pp. 311–335). Mahwah, NJ: Lawrence Erlbaum Associates.

Goldstein, B., Harris, K., & Klein, M. (1993). Assessment of oral storytelling abilities of Latino junior high school students with learning handicaps. *Journal of Learning Disabilities, 26,* 138–143. doi: 10.1177/002221949302600207

Gottardo, A. (2002). Language and reading skills in bilingual Spanish-English speakers. *Topics in Language Disorders, 23,* 42–66.

Gottlieb, M., Cranley, M.E., & Oliver, A.R. (2007). *WIDA (World-Class Instructional Design and Assessment) consortium: English language proficiency standards and resource guide.* Madison: University of Wisconsin.

Graves, A.W. (1986). Effects of direct instruction and metacomprehension training of finding main ideas. *Learning Disabilities Research and Practice, 1,* 90–100.

Graves, M.F. (2000). A vocabulary program to complement and bolster a middle-grade comprehension program. In B.M. Taylor, M.F. Graves, & P. Van Den Broek (Eds.), *Reading for meaning: Fostering comprehension in the middle grades* (pp. 116–135). New York, NY: Teachers College Press.

Graves, M.F. (2006). *The vocabulary book.* New York, NY: Teachers College Press.

Griffin, C.C., & Tulbert, B. (1995). The effect of graphic organizers on students' comprehension and recall of expository texts. *Reading and Writing Quarterly, 11,* 73–89.

Gunn, T.M. (2008). The effects of questioning on text processing. *Reading Psychology, 29,* 405–442.

Guthrie, J. (2008). *Engaging adolescents in reading.* Thousand Oaks, CA: Corwin Press.

Guthrie, J.T., Mcrae, A., & Klauda, S.L. (2007). Contributions of concept-oriented reading instruction to knowledge about interventions for motivations in reading. *Educational Psychologist, 42,* 237–250. doi:10.1080/00461520701621087

Guthrie, J.T., Wigfield, A., Barbosa, P., Perencevich, K.C., Taboada, A., Davis, M., . . . Tonks, S. (2004). Increasing reading comprehension and engagement through concept-oriented reading instruction. *Journal of Educational Psychology, 96,* 403–423. doi:10.1037/0022-0663.96.3.403

Guthrie, J.T., Wigfield, A., & You, W. (2012). Instructional contexts for engagement and achievement in reading. In S.L. Christenson & A.L. Reschley (Eds.), *Handbook on research on student engagement* (pp. 601–634). doi: 10.1007/978-1-4614-2018-7_29

Guzzetti, B., & Hynd, C. (Eds.). (1998). *Theoretical perspectives on conceptual change.* Mahwah, NJ: Lawrence Erlbaum Associates.

Hall, L.A. (2004). Comprehending expository text: Promising strategies for struggling readers and students with reading disabilities. *Reading Research and Instruction, 44,* 75–95.

Hallahan, D.P., Lloyd, J.W., Kauffman, J.M., Weiss, M.P., & Martinez, E.A. (2005). *Learning disabilities: Foundations, characteristics, and effective teaching* (3rd ed.). Boston, MA: Pearson.

Hamayan, E.V., Marler, B., Sanchez-Lopez, C., & Damico, J.S. (2007). *Some myths regarding ELLs and special education.* Retrieved from http://www.colorincolorado.org/article/40714/

Harniss, M.K., Dickson, S.V., Kinder, D., & Hollenbeck, K.L. (2001). Textual problems and instructional solutions: Strategies for enhancing learning from published history textbooks. *Reading and Writing Quarterly, 17,* 127–150.

Harris, K.R., Graham, S., Mason, L.H., & Friedlander, B. (2008). *Powerful writing strategies for all students.* Baltimore, MD: Paul H. Brookes Publishing Co.

Hart, B., & Risley, T.R. (1995). *Meaningful differences in the everyday experience of young American children.* Baltimore, MD: Paul H. Brookes Publishing Co.

Harvey, S., & Goudvis, A. (2000). *Strategies that work: Teaching comprehension to enhance understanding.* York, ME: Stenhouse Publishers.

Heath, S.B. (1982). What no bedtime story means: Narrative skills at home and school. *Language in Society, 11,* 49–76.

Heller, R., & Greenleaf, C. (2007). *Literacy instruction in the content areas: Getting to the core of middle and high school improvement.* Washington, DC: Alliance for Excellent Education.

Hiebert, E.J., Winograd, P.N., & Danner, F.W. (1984). Children's attributions for failure and success in different aspects of reading. *Journal of Educational Psychology, 76,* 1139–1148.

Hindman, A.H., Erhart, A.C., & Wasik, B.A. (2012). Reducing the Matthew Effect: Lessons from the ExCELL head start intervention. *Early Education and Development, 23,* 781–806.

Hoare, B. (2003). *Parasites and partners: Breeders.* Chicago, IL: Raintree.

Hock, M.F., Schumaker, J.B., & Deshler, D.D. (1999). Closing the gap to success in secondary schools: A model for cognitive apprenticeship. In D.D. Deshler, J. Schumaker, K.R. Harris, & S. Graham (Eds.), *Teaching every adolescent every day: Learning in diverse middle and high school classrooms* (pp. 1–52). Brookline, MA: Brookline Books.

Individuals with Disabilities Education Improvement Act (IDEA) of 2004, PL 108-446, 20 U.S.C. §§ 1400 *et seq.*

Institute of Education Sciences. (2010). *Improving reading comprehension in kindergarten through 3rd grade: What works clearinghouse* (IES Practice Guide No. NCEE 2010-4038). Retrieved from http://ies.ed.gov/ncee/wwc/practiceguide.aspx?sid=14

International Reading Association. (2007). *Key issues and questions in English language learners literacy research.* Newark, DE: International Reading Association and Washington, DC: International Institute of Child Health and Human Development.

Ivey, G. (2002). Getting started: Manageable practices. *Educational Leadership, 60*(3), 20–23.

Jacobs, J.E., Lanza, S., Osgood, D.W., Eccles, J.S., & Wigfield, A. (2002). Changes in children's self-competence and values: Gender and domain differences across grades one through twelve. *Child Development, 73,* 509–527.

Jennings, J.H., Caldwell, J.S., & Lerner, J.W. (2010). *Reading problems: Assessment and teaching strategies* (6th ed.). Boston, MA: Pearson.

Jitendra, A.K., Edwards, L.L., Sacks, G., & Jacobson, L.A. (2004). What research says about vocabulary instruction for students with learning disabilities. *Exceptional Children, 70,* 299–322.

Jitendra, A.K., & Gajria, M. (2011). Reading comprehension instruction for students with learning disabilities. *Focus on Exceptional Children, 43*(8), 1–16.

Jitendra, A.K., Hoppes, M.K., & Xin, Y.P. (2000). Enhancing main idea comprehension for students with learning problems: The role of a summarization strategy and self-monitoring instruction. *Journal of Special Education, 34,* 127–139.

Jitendra, A.K., Nolet, V., Xin, Y.P., Gomez, O., Iskold, L., Renouf, K., & DaCosta, J. (2001). An analysis of middle school geography textbooks: Implications for students with learning problems. *Reading and Writing Quarterly, 17,* 151–174. doi: 10.1080/10573 5601300007606

Johnson, E., Mellard, D.F., Fuchs, D., & McKnight, M.A. (2006). *Responsiveness to intervention (RTI): How to do it.* Lawrence, KS: National Research Center on Learning Disabilities.

Jonassen, D.H., & Grabowski, B.L. (1993). *Handbook of individual differences, learning, and instruction: Part VII, Prior Knowledge.* Mahwah, NJ: Lawrence Erlbaum Associates.

Jones, B.F., Palincsar, A.S., Ogle, D.S., & Carr, E.G. (1987). *Strategic teaching and learning: Cognitive instruction in the content areas.* Alexandria, VA: Association for Supervision and Curriculum Development.

Joseph, L.M., & Schisler, R. (2009). Should adolescents go back to the basics? A review of teaching word reading skills to middle and high school students. *Remedial and Special Education, 30,* 131–147.

Judge, S., & Bell, S.M. (2011). Reading achievement trajectories for students with learning disabilities during the elementary years. *Reading and Writing Quarterly, 27,* 153–178.

Katz, L.A., Stone, C.A., Carlisle, J.F., Corey, D., & Zeng, J. (2008). Initial progress of children identified with disabilities in Michigan's Reading-First schools. *Exceptional Children, 74,* 235–256.

Keene, E.O. (2008). *To understand: New horizons in reading comprehension.* Portsmouth, NH: Heinemann.

Keene, E.O., & Zimmerman, S. (2007). *Mosaic of thought: The power of comprehension strategy instruction* (2nd ed.). Portsmouth, NH: Heinemann.

Kennedy, M.J., & Deshler, D.D. (2010). Literacy instruction, technology, and students with learning disabilities: Research we have, research we need. *Learning Disability Quarterly, 3,* 289–298.

Kieffer, M.J., & Lesaux, N.K. (2008). The role of derivational morphological awareness in the reading comprehension of Spanish-speaking English language learners. *Reading and Writing: An Interdisciplinary Journal, 21,* 783–804.

Kieffer, M.J., & Lesaux, N.K. (2012). Development of morphological awareness and vocabulary knowledge for Spanish-speaking language minority learners: A parallel process latent growth model. *Applied Psycholinguistics, 33,* 23–54.

Kim, A., Vaughn, S., Wanzek, J., & Wei, S. (2004). Graphic organizers and their effects on the reading comprehension of students with LD: A synthesis of research. *Journal of Learning Disabilities, 37,* 105–118.

Kintsch, W., & Kintsch, E. (2005). Comprehension. In S.G. Paris & S.A. Stahl (Eds.), *Children's reading: Comprehension and assessment* (pp. 71–92). Mahwah, NJ: Lawrence Erlbaum Associates.

Klassen, R.M. (2006). Too much confidence? The self-efficacy of adolescents with learning disabilities. In F. Pajares & T. Urdan (Eds.), *Self-efficacy beliefs of adolescents* (pp. 181–200). Greenwich, CT: Information Age Publishing.

Klingner, J.K., & Vaughn, S. (1998). Using collaborative strategic reading. *Teaching Exceptional Children, 30,* 32–37.

Klingner, J.K., Vaughn, S., & Boardman, A. (2007). *Teaching reading comprehension to students with learning difficulties.* New York, NY: Guilford Press.

Klingner, J.K., Vaughn, S., & Schumm, J.S. (1998). Collaborative strategic reading during social studies in heterogeneous fourth-grade classrooms. *Elementary School Journal, 99,* 3–22.

Krashen, S.D. (1982). *Principles and practice in second language acquisition.* Retrieved from http://sdkrashen.com/

Kuo, L., & Anderson, R.C. (2006). Morphological awareness and learning to read: A cross-language perspective. *Educational Psychologist, 41,* 161–180.

Lajoie, S.P. (2008). Metacognition, self-regulation, and self-regulated learning: A rose by any other name? *Educational Psychology Review, 20,* 469–475.

Lanauze, M., & Snow, C. (1989). The relation between first- and second- language writing skills: Evidence from Puerto Rican elementary school children in bilingual programs. *Linguistics and Education, 1,* 323–339. doi: 10.1016/S0898-5898(89)80005-1

Larsen-Freeman, D., & Long, M.H. (1991). *An introduction to second language acquisition research.* New York, NY: Longman.

Lau, K.L. (2009). Reading motivation, perceptions of reading instruction and reading amount: A comparison of junior and senior secondary students in Hong Kong. *Journal of Research in Reading, 32,* 366–382. doi:10.1111/j.1467-9817.2009.01400.x

Lee, J., & Schallert, D.L. (1997). The relative contribution of L2 language proficiency and L1 reading ability to L2 reading performance: A test of the threshold hypothesis in an EFL context. *TESOL Quarterly, 31,* 713–739.

Lenz, B.K., Ellis, E.S., & Scanlon, D. (1996). *Teaching learning strategies to adolescents and adults with learning disabilities.* Austin, TX: PRO-ED.

Lerner, J.W., & Johns, B. (2009). *Learning disabilities and related mild disabilities: Characteristics, teaching strategies and new directions.* Florence, KY: Cengage Learning.

Lesaux, N.K., & Marietta, S.H. (2012). *Making assessments matter: Using test results to differentiate reading instruction.* New York, NY: Guilford Press.

Levy, B.A., Abello, B., & Lysynchuk, L. (1997). Transfer from word training to reading in context: Gains in reading fluency and comprehension. *Learning Disability Quarterly, 20,* 173–188.

Licht, B.G., Kistener, J.A., Ozkaragoz, T., Shapiro, S., & Clausen, L. (1985). Causal attributions of learning disabled children: Individual differences and their implications for persistence. *Journal of Educational Psychology, 77,* 208–216.

Linnenbrink, E.A., & Pintrich, P.R. (2003). The role of self-efficacy beliefs in student engagement and learning in the classroom. *Reading and Writing Quarterly, 19,* 119–137.

Lovett, M.W., Lacerenza, L., DePalma, M., Benson, N.J., Steinback, K.A., & Frijters, J.C. (2008). Preparing teachers to remediate reading disabilities in high school: What is needed for effective professional development? *Teaching and Teacher Education, 24,* 1083–1097.

Lovitt, T.C., & Horton, S.V. (1994). Strategies for adapting science textbooks for youth with learning disabilities. *Remedial and Special Education, 15,* 105–116. doi: 10.177/074193259401500206

Lyon, G.R., Alexander, D., & Yaffe, S. (1997). Progress and promise in research: Learning Disabilities. *Learning Disabilities: A Multidisciplinary Journal, 8,* 1–6.

Malone, L.D., & Mastropieri, M.A. (1992). Reading comprehension instruction: Summarization and self-monitoring training for students with learning disabilities. *Exceptional Children, 58,* 270–279.

Mancilla-Martinez, J., & Lesaux, N.K. (2011). The gap between Spanish speakers' word reading and word knowledge: A longitudinal study. *Child Development, 82,* 1544–1560.

Manis, F.R., Lindsey, K.A., & Bailey, C.E. (2004). Development of reading in grades K–2 in Spanish-speaking English-language learners. *Learning Disabilities Research and Practice, 19,* 214–224. doi: 10.1111/j.1540-5826.2004.00107.x

Marzano, R.J., Norford, J.S., Paynter, D.E., Pickering, D.J., & Gaddy, B.B. (2001). *A handbook for classroom instruction that works.* Alexandria, VA: Association for Supervision and Curriculum Development.

Mastropieri, M.A., & Scruggs, T.E. (1991). *Teaching students ways to remember: Strategies for learning mnemonically.* Brookline, MA: Brookline Books.

Mastropieri, M.A., & Scruggs, T.E. (1997). Best practices in promoting reading comprehension in students with learning disabilities: 1976 to 1996. *Remedial and Special Education, 18,* 197–213.

Mastropieri, M.A., & Scruggs, T.E. (2010). *The inclusive classroom: Strategies for effective instruction* (4th ed.). Upper Saddle River, NJ: Pearson.

Mastropieri, M.A., Scruggs, T.E., & Graetz, J.E. (2003). Reading comprehension instruction for secondary students: Challenges for struggling students and teachers. *Learning Disabilities Quarterly, 26,* 103–117. doi:10.2307/1593593

McEwan, E.K. (2008). *The reading puzzle: Word analysis.* Thousand Oaks, CA: Corwin Press.

McKeown, M.G., Beck, I.L., Omanson, R.C., & Pople, M.T. (1985). Some effects of the nature and frequency of vocabulary instruction on the knowledge and use of words. *Reading Research Quarterly, 20,* 522–535.

Meece, J.L., Blumenfeld, P.C., & Hoyle, R.H. (1988). Students' goal orientations and cognitive engagement in classroom activities. *Journal of Educational Psychology, 80,* 514–523. doi:10.1037/0022-0663.80.4.514

Mercer, C.D., & Mercer, A.R. (2005). *Teaching students with learning problems* (7th ed.). Upper Saddle River, NJ: Prentice Hall.

Methe, S.A., & Hintze, J.M. (2003). Evaluating teacher modeling as a strategy to improve silent reading. *School Psychology Review, 32,* 617–622.

Meyer, B.J.F., & Ray, M.N. (2011). Structure strategy interventions: Increasing reading comprehension of expository text. *International Electronic Journal of Elementary Education (Special Issue on Reading Comprehension), 4,* 127–152.

Moats, L.C. (2010). *Speech to print: Language essentials for teachers* (2nd ed.). Baltimore, MD: Paul H. Brookes Publishing Co.

Moll, L.C. (1989). Teaching second language students: A Vygotskian approach. In D. Johnson & D. Roen, (Eds.), *Richness in writing: Empowering ESL students* (pp. 55–69). New York, NY: Longman.

Moll, L.C., Amanti, C., Neff, D., & González, N. (1992). Funds of knowledge for teaching: A qualitative approach to connect households and classrooms. *Theory Into Practice, 31,* 132–141.

Moll, L.C., & González, N. (1994). Lessons from research with language minority students. *Journal of Reading Behavior, 26,* 439–461. (Reprinted in Cushman, E., Kintgen, E., Kroll, B., & Rose, M. [Eds.]. [2001]. *Literacy: A critical sourcebook.* Boston, MA: Bedford/St. Martin's.)

Morgan, P.L., Fuchs, D., Compton, D.L., Cordray, D.S., & Fuchs, L.S. (2008). Does early reading failure decrease children's reading motivation? *Journal of Learning Disabilities, 41,* 387–404.

Morrone, A.S., & Pintrich, P.R. (2006). Achievement motivation. In G.G. Bear & K.M. Minke (Eds.), *Children's needs III: Development, prevention, and intervention.* Washington, DC: National Association of Secondary School Principals.

Nagy, W. (1988). *Teaching vocabulary to improve reading comprehension.* Newark, DE: International Reading Association.

Nagy, W. (1997). On the role of the context in first- and second-language vocabulary learning. In N. Schmitt & M. McCarthy (Eds.), *Vocabulary: Description, acquisition and pedagogy* (pp. 64–83). Cambridge, United Kingdom: Cambridge University Press.

Nagy, W., & Anderson, R. (1984). The number of words in printed school English. *Reading Research Quarterly, 19,* 304–330.

Nagy, W.E., Berninger, V.W., & Abbott, R.D. (2006). Contributions of morphology beyond phonology to literacy outcomes of upper elementary and middle-school students. *Journal of Educational Psychology, 98,* 134–147.

Nagy, W.E., García, G.E., Durgunoglu, A.Y., & Hancin-Bhatt, B. (1993). Spanish-English bilingual students' use of cognates in English reading. *Journal of Reading Behavior, 25,* 241–259. doi: 10.1080/10862969009547816

Nagy, W.E., & Scott, J.A. (2000). Vocabulary processes. In M.L. Kamil, P. Mosenthal, P.D. Pearson, & R. Barr (Eds.), *Handbook of reading research* (Vol. 3, pp. 269–284). Mahwah, NJ: Lawrence Erlbaum Associates.

National Center for Education Statistics. (2011). *National Assessment of Educational Progress (NAEP) 2011 reading assessment.* Retrieved from http://nces.ed.gov/nationsreportcard/reading/

National Center for Educational Statistics. (2012). *The condition of education.* Washington, DC: Institute of Education Sciences, U.S. Department of Education.

National Center for Learning Disabilities. (2013). *The history of learning disabilities.* Retrieved from http://www.ncld.org

National Institute of Child Health and Human Development. (2000). *Teaching children to read: An evidence-based assessment of the scientific research literature on reading and its implications for reading instruction.* Retrieved from http://www.nichd.nih.gov/publications/nrp/smallbook.cfm

National Reading Panel. (2000). *Put reading first: The research building blocks for teaching children to read.* Jessup, MD: Author.

National Research Council. (2000). *How people learn: Bridging research and practice.* Washington, DC: National Academies Press.

National Research Council. (2004). *Engaging schools: Fostering high school students' motivation to learn.* Washington, DC: National Academies Press.

Nelson, J.M., & Manset-Williamson, G. (2006). The impact of explicit, self-regulatory reading comprehension strategy instruction on the reading-specific self-efficacy, attributions, and affect of students with reading disabilities. *Learning Disability Quarterly, 29,* 213–230.

Oczkus, L. (2004). *Super 6 comprehension strategies: 35 lessons and more for reading success.* Norwood, MA: Christopher-Gordon Publishers.

Ogle, D. (1986). K-W-L: A teaching model that develops active reading of expository text. *The Reading Teacher, 39,* 564–570.

Olivier, M.A.J., & Steenkamp, D.S. (2004). Attention deficit/hyperactivity disorder: Underlying deficits in achievement motivation. *International Journal for the Advancement of Counseling, 26,* 47–63.

Otero, J.C., & Kintsch, W. (1992). Failures to detect contradictions in a text: What readers believe versus what they read. *Psychological Science, 3,* 229–235.

Pace, A.J., Marshall, N., Horowitz, R., Lipson, M.Y., & Lucido, P. (1989). When prior knowledge doesn't facilitate some text comprehension: An examination of some of the issues. In S. McCormick & J. Zutell (Eds.), *Cognitive and social perspectives for literacy research and instruction: Thirty-eighth yearbook of the national reading conference* (pp. 213–224). Chicago, IL: National Reading Conference.

Pajares, F. (2006). Self-efficacy during childhood and adolescence: Implications for teachers and parents. In F. Pajares & T. Urdan (Eds.), *Self-efficacy beliefs of adolescents* (pp. 339–367). Greenwich, CT: Information Age Publishing.

Pajares, F., & Kranzler, J. (1995). Self-efficacy beliefs and general mental ability in mathematical problem-solving. *Contemporary Educational Psychology, 20,* 426–443. doi:10.1006/ceps.1995.1029

Paris, S.G., Lipson, M.Y., & Wixson, K.K. (1983). Becoming a strategic reader. *Contemporary Educational Psychology, 8,* 293–316.

Paris, S.G., & Oka, E.R. (1986). Children's reading strategies, metacognition and motivation. *Developmental Review, 6,* 25–56.

Paris, S.G., & Winograd, P. (1990). How metacognition can promote academic learning and instruction. In B.F. Jones & L. Idol (Eds.), *Dimensions of thinking and cognitive instruction* (pp. 15–51). Mahwah, NJ: Lawrence Erlbaum Associates.

Pearson, P.D., & Cervetti, G. (2012). *The psychology and pedagogy of reading processes.* Retrieved from http://onlinelibrary.wiley.com/doi/10.1002/9781118133880.hop207012/abstract

Peregoy, S. (1989). Relationships between second language oral proficiency and reading comprehension of bilingual fifth grade students. *Journal of the National Association for Bilingual Education, 13*(3), 217–234. Retrieved from http://www.eric.ed.gov/ERICWebPortal/detail?accno=EJ436517

Perencevich, K.C. (2004). *The associations of autonomy support and conceptual press with engaged reading and conceptual learning from text.* College Park: University of Maryland.

Phythian-Sence, C., & Wagner, R.K. (2007). Vocabulary acquisition: A primer. In R.K. Wagner, A.E. Muse, & K.R. Tannenbaum (Eds.), *Vocabulary acquisition: Implications for reading comprehension* (pp. 1–14). New York, NY: Guilford Press.

Power de-Fur, L. (2011). *Special education eligibility: When is a speech-language impairment also a disability?* Retrieved from http://www.asha.org/Publications/leader/2011/110405/

Pressley, M., & Afflerbach, P. (1995). *Verbal protocols of reading: The nature of constructively responsive reading.* Mahwah, NJ: Lawrence Erlbaum Associates.

Pressley, M., Almasi, J., Schuder, T., Bergman, J., Hite, S., El-Dinary, P.B., & Brown, R. (1994). Transactional instruction of comprehension strategies: The Montgomery County, Maryland, SAIL program. *Reading and Writing Quarterly: Overcoming Learning Difficulties, 10,* 5–19.

Pressley, M., & Ghatala, E.S. (1990). Self-regulated learning: Monitoring learning from text. *Educational Psychologist, 25,* 19–33.

Proctor, C.P., Carlo, M.S., August, D., & Snow, C.E. (2006). Native Spanish-speaking children reading in English: Toward a model of comprehension. *Journal of Educational Psychology, 97,* 246–256.

Pullen, P.C., & Cash, D.B. (2011). Reading. In J.M. Kauffman, & D.P. Hallahan (Eds.), *Handbook of special education* (pp. 409–421). New York, NY; Routledge.

Pullen, P.C., Lane, H.B., Ashworth, K.A., & Lovelace, S.P. (2011). Learning disabilities. In J.M. Kauffman & D.P. Hallahan (Eds.), *Handbook of special education* (pp. 187–197). New York, NY; Routledge.

Quiroga, T., Lemos-Britton, Z., Mostafapour, E., Abbot, R.D., & Berninger, V.W. (2002). Phono-logical awareness and beginning reading in Spanish-speaking ESL first graders: Research into practice. *Journal of School Psychology, 40,* 85–111.

Rasinski, T.V., Padak, N., Newton, J., & Newton, E. (2011). The Latin-Greek connection build-ing vocabulary through morphological study. *The Reading Teacher, 65,* 133–141.

Reese, L., Garnier, H., Gallimore, R., & Goldenberg, C. (2000). Longitudinal analysis of the antecedents of emergent Spanish literacy and middle-school English reading achievement of Spanish-speaking students. *American Educational Research Journal, 37,* 633–662.

Regan, K., & Berkeley, S. (2012). Effective reading and writing instruction: A focus on mod-eling. *Intervention in School and Clinic, 47,* 276–282.

Regan, K., Berkeley, S., Hughes, M., & Kirby, S. (2013). Computer-assisted instruction for struggling elementary readers with learning disabilities. *Journal of Special Education, first published on August 16, 2013 as doi:10.1177/0022466913497261*

Reynolds, P.L., & Symons, S. (2001). Motivational variables and children's text search. *Jour-nal of Educational Psychology, 93,* 14–22. doi:10.1037//0022-0663.93.1.14

Roberts, G., Torgesen, J.K., Boardman, A., & Scammacca, N. (2008). Evidenced-based strate-gies for reading instruction of older students with learning disabilities. *Learning Disabil-ities Research and Practice, 23,* 63–69.

Roberts, K.L., & Duke, N.K. (2010). Comprehension in the elementary grades: The research base. In K. Ganske & D. Fisher (Eds.), *Comprehension across the curriculum: Perspec-tives and practices K–12* (pp. 23–45). New York, NY: Guilford Press.

Robinson, F.P. (1961). *Effective study* (Rev. ed.). New York, NY: Harper & Row.

Roth, F.P., Speece, D.L., & Cooper, D.H. (2002). A longitudinal analysis of the connection between oral language and early reading. *Journal of Educational Research, 95,* 259–272.

Royer, J., & Carlo, M. (1991). Transfer of comprehension skills from native to second language. *Journal of Reading, 34,* 450–455.

Rumelhart, D.E. (1984). Schemata and the cognitive system. In R.S. Wyer & T.K. Srull (Eds.), *Handbook of social cognition* (Vol. 1, pp. 161–188). Mahwah, NJ: Lawrence Erlbaum Associates.

Rumelhart, D.E. (1994). Toward an interactive model of reading. In R.B. Ruddell, M.R. Rud-dell, & H. Singer (Eds.), *Theoretical models and processes of reading* (4th ed., pp. 864–894). Newark, DE: International Reading Association.

Rupley, W.H., Blair, T.R., & Nichols, W.D. (2009). Effective reading instruction for struggling readers: The role of direct/explicit teaching. *Reading and Writing Quarterly, 25,* 125–138.

Saenz, L.M., & Fuchs, L.S. (2002). Examining the reading difficulties of secondary students with learning disabilities: Expository versus narrative texts. *Remedial and Special Edu-cation, 23,* 31–41.

Sampson, M.B., Rasinski, T.V., & Sampson, M. (2003). *Total literacy: Reading, writing, and learning* (3rd ed.). Belmont, CA: Wadsworth/Thomson Learning.

Santella, A. (2001). *The Lakota Sioux.* New York, NY: Scholastic Inc.

Scardamalia, M., Bereiter, C., & Lamon, M. (1994). CSILE: Trying to bring students into world 3. In K. McGilley (Ed.), *Classroom lessons: Integrating cognitive theory and classroom practice* (pp. 201–228). Cambridge, MA: The MIT Press.

Schiefele, U. (1999). Interest and learning from text. *Scientific Studies of Reading, 3,* 257–279.

Schleppegrell, M.J. (2004). *The language of schooling: A functional linguistics perspec-tive.* Mahwah, NJ: Lawrence Erlbaum Associates.

Schumaker, J.B., Denton, P.H., & Deshler, D.D. (1984). *The learning strategies curricu-lum: The paraphrasing strategy.* Lawrence: University of Kansas, Center for Research on Learning.

Schunk, D.H. (1985). Self-efficacy and classroom learning. *Psychology in the Schools, 22,* 208–223.

Schunk, D.H. (1991). Goal setting and self-evaluation: A social cognitive perspective on self-regulation. In M.L. Maehr & P.R. Pintrich (Eds.), *Advances in motivation and achieve-ment: Goals and self-regulatory processes* (Vol. 7, pp. 85–113). Greenwich, CT: JAI Press.

Schunk, D.H., & Cox, P.D. (1986). Strategic training and attributional feedback with learning disabled students. *Journal of Educational Psychology, 78,* 201–209.

Schunk, D.H., & Miller, S.D. (2002). Self-efficacy and adolescents' motivation. In F. Pajares & T. Urdan (Eds.), *Academic motivation of adolescents* (pp. 29–52). Greenwich, CT: Information Age.

Scruggs, T.E., & Mastropieri, M.A. (2002). On babies and bathwater. *Learning Disability Quarterly, 25,* 155–168.

Segretto, M. (2002). *Roadmap to 8th grade reading: Virginia edition.* New York, NY: Princeton Review Publishing.

Sejnost, R.L., & Thiese, S.M. (2010). *Building content literacy.* Thousand Oaks, CA: Corwin Press.

Shaywitz, S. (2003). *Overcoming dyslexia: A new and complete science-based program for reading problems at any level.* New York, NY: Alfred A. Knopf.

Shaywitz, S., Morris, R., & Shaywitz, B. (2008). The education of dyslexic children from childhood to young adulthood. *Annual Review of Psychology, 50,* 451–475.

Shaywitz, S., & Shaywitz, B. (1998). Functional disruption in the organization of the brain in reading for dyslexia. *Proceedings of the National Academy of Sciences, 95,* 5.

Shell, D., Colvin, C., & Bruning, R. (1995). Self-efficacy, attribution and outcome expectancy mechanisms in reading and writing achievement: Grade-level and achievement-level differences. *Journal of Educational Psychology, 87,* 386–398.

Sideridis, G.D., & Scanlon, D. (2006). Motivational issues in learning disabilities. *Learning Disability Quarterly, 29,* 131–135.

Skinner, E.A., Kindermann, T., & Furrer, C. (2009). A motivational perspective on engagement and disaffection: Conceptualization and assessment of children's behavioral and emotional participation in academic activities in the classroom. *Educational and Psychological Measurement, 69,* 493–525. doi:10.1177/0013164408323233

Smey-Richman, B. (1991). At-risk, low-achieving students: Characteristics and instructional implications. *Equity and Excellence in Education, 25,* 25–29.

Snow, C.E., & Kim, Y.S. (2007). Large problem spaces: The challenge of vocabulary for English language learners. In R.K. Wagner, A.E. Muse, & K.R. Tannenbaum (Eds.), *Vocabulary acquisition: Implications for reading comprehension* (pp. 123–139). New York, NY: Guilford Press.

Stahl, S.A. (1999). *Vocabulary development.* Brookline, MA: Brookline Books.

Stahl, S.A., & Nagy, W.E. (2006). *Teaching word meanings.* Mahwah, NJ: Lawrence Erlbaum Associates.

Stanovich, K.E. (1986). Matthew Effects in reading: Some consequences of individual differences in the acquisition of literacy. *Reading Research Quarterly, 21,* 360–407.

Stanovich, K.E., Cunningham, A.E., & Freeman, D.J. (1984). Intelligence, cognitive skills and early reading progress. *Reading Research Quarterly, 19,* 278–303.

Stefanou, C.R., Perencevich, K.C., DiCintio, M., & Turner, J.C. (2004). Supporting autonomy in the classroom: Ways teachers encourage student decision making and ownership. *Educational Psychologist, 39*(2), 97–110. doi:10.1207/s15326985ep3902_2

Stipek, D.J. (1993). *Motivation to learn: From theory to practice* (2nd ed.). Boston, MA: Allyn & Bacon.

Stipek, D.J., & Tannatt, L.M. (1984). Children's judgments of their own and their peers' academic competence. *Journal of Educational Psychology, 76,* 75–84.

Stipek, D.J., & Weiz, J.R. (1981). Perceived personal control and academic achievement. *Review of Educational Research, 51,* 101–137.

Swanson, H.L. (1999). Reading research for students with LD: A meta-analysis of intervention outcomes. *Journal of Learning Disabilities, 32,* 504–532. doi:10.1177/002221949903200605

Swanson, H.L., & Hoskyn, M. (1998). Experimental intervention research on students with learning disabilities: A meta-analysis of treatment outcomes. *Review of Educational Research, 68,* 277–321. doi:10.3102/00346543068003277

Swanson, H.L., & Hoskyn, M. (2001). Instructing adolescents with learning disabilities: A component and composite analysis. *Learning Disabilities Research and Practice, 16,* 109–119.

Tabassam, W., & Grainger, J. (2002). Self-concept, attributional style and self-efficacy beliefs of students with learning disabilities with and without attention deficit hyperactivity disorder. *Learning Disability Quarterly, 25,* 141–151.

Taboada, A. (2012). Relationships of general vocabulary, academic vocabulary, and student questioning with reading comprehension in students with varying levels of English proficiency. *Instructional Science, 40,* 901–923. doi: 10.1007/s11251-011-9196-z

Taboada, A., & Guthrie, J.T. (2004). Growth of cognitive strategies for reading comprehension. In J.T. Guthrie, A. Wigfield, & K. Perencevich (Eds.), *Motivating reading comprehension: Concept-oriented reading instruction* (pp. 273–306). Mahwah, NJ: Lawrence Erlbaum Associates.

Taboada, A., & Guthrie, J.T. (2006). Contributions of student questioning and prior knowledge to construction of knowledge from reading information text. *Journal of Literacy Research, 38,* 1–35.

Taboada, A., & Rutherford, V. (2011). Developing reading comprehension and academic vocabulary for English language learners through science content: A formative experiment. *Reading Psychology, 32,* 113–157. doi:10.1080/02702711003604468

Taboada Barber, A., Buehl, M.M, Kidd, J.K., Sturtevant, E., Richey, L.N., & Beck, J. (in press). Engagement in social studies: Exploring the role of a social studies literacy intervention on reading comprehension, reading self-efficacy, and engagement in middle school students with different language backgrounds. *Reading Psychology.*

Taboada Barber, A., Richey, L., & Buehl, M.M. (2013). Promoting comprehension and motivation to read in the middle school social studies classroom: Examples from a research-based curriculum. In R.T. Boon & V. Spencer (Eds.), *Adolescent literacy: Strategies for content comprehension in inclusive classrooms* (pp. 13–28). Baltimore, MD: Paul H. Brookes Publishing Co.

Taylor, B.M., Pearson, P.D., Clark, K., & Walpole, S. (2000). Effective schools and accomplished teachers: Lessons about primary-grade reading instruction in low-income schools. *Elementary School Journal, 101,* 121–165.

Taylor, B.M., & Williams, J.P. (1983). Children's use of text structure in the recall of expository material. *Reading Research Quarterly, 19,* 134–146.

Thompson, G. (1998). *Animals in danger.* Austin, TX: Steck-Vaughn Company.

Torgesen, J.K., Houston, D.D., Rissman, L.M., Decker, S.M., Roberts, G., Vaughn, S., . . . Lesaux, N. (2007). *Academic literacy instruction for adolescents: A guidance document from the center on instruction.* Portsmouth, NH: RMC Research Corporation, Center on Instruction.

Tovani, C. (2004). *Do I really have to teach reading?* Portland, ME: Stenhouse Publishers.

U.S. Department of Education. (2003). *Twenty-fifth annual report to Congress on the implementation of the Individuals with Disabilities Act.* Washington, DC: Author.

U.S. Department of Education. (2009). *The condition of education 2009.* Retrieved from http://www.nces.ed.gov/pubsearch/pubsinfo.asp?pubid=2009081

Valas, H. (1999). Students with learning disabilities and low achieving students: Peer acceptance, loneliness, self-esteem, and depression. *Social Psychology of Education, 3,* 173–192.

Vaughn, S., & Bos, C.S. (2009). *Strategies for teaching students with learning and behavior problems* (7th ed.). Boston, MA: Allyn & Bacon.

Vaughn, S., Gersten, R., & Chard, D. (2000). The underlying message in LD interventions research. *Exceptional Children, 67,* 99–114.

Vidal-Abarca, E., Martinez, G., & Gilabert, R. (2000). Two procedures to improve instructional text: Effects on memory and learning. *Journal of Educational Psychology, 92,* 107–116. doi:10.1037//0022-0663.92.1.107

Wagner, R.K., & Torgesen, J.K. (1987). The nature of phonological processing and its causal role in the acquisition of reading skills. *Psychological Bulletin, 101,* 192–212.

Walberg, H.J., & Tsai, S. (1983). Matthew Effect in education. *American Educational Research Journal, 20,* 359–373.

Walker, B.J. (2003). The cultivation of student self-efficacy in reading and writing. *Reading and Writing Quarterly, 19,* 173–187.

Weiner, B. (1974). *Achievement motivation and attribution theory.* Morristown, NJ: General Learning Press.

Weiner, B. (1979). A theory of motivation for some classroom experiences. *Journal of Educational Psychology, 71,* 3–25.

Weiner, B. (1980). *Human motivation.* Austin, TX: Holt, Rinehart & Winston.

Weiner, B. (1985). An attributional theory of achievement motivation and emotion. *Psychological Review, 92,* 548–573.

Weiner, B. (1986). *An attributional theory of motivation and emotion.* New York, NY: Springer Verlag.

Wiley, J., Griffin, T.D., & Thiede, K.W. (2005). Putting the comprehension in metacomprehension. *Journal of General Psychology, 132,* 408–428.

Williams, J.P. (1993). Comprehension of students with and without learning disabilities: Identification of narrative themes and idiosyncratic text representations. *Journal of Educational Psychology, 93,* 631–641.

Williams, J.P. (1998). Improving the comprehension of disabled readers. *Annals of Dyslexia, 48,* 213–238.

Wixson, K.K., & Lipson, M.Y. (1991). Perspectives on reading disability research. In R. Barr, M. Kamil, P. Mosenthal, & P.D. Pearson (Eds.), *Handbook of reading research* (Vol. II, pp. 539–570). New York, NY: Longman.

Wong, B.Y.L. (1980). Activating the inactive learner: Use of questions/prompts to enhance comprehension and retention of implied information in learning disabled children. *Learning Disability Quarterly, 3,* 29–37.

Wong, B.Y.L. (2004). *Learning about learning disabilities* (3rd ed.). San Diego, CA: Academic Press.

Woodruff, S., Schumaker, J.B., & Deshler, D.D. (2002). *The effects of an intensive reading intervention on the decoding skills of high school students with reading deficits.* Lawrence: University of Kansas Institute for Academic Access.

Wren, S. (n.d.) *Developing research-based resources for the balanced reading teacher.* Austin, TX: Author. Retrieved from http://www.balancedreading.com

Wren, S. (2003). *Matthew Effects in reading.* Retrieved from http://www.balancedreading.com/matthew.html

Xu, S.H. (2010). *Teaching English language learners: Literacy strategies and resources for K–6.* New York, NY: Guilford Press.

Zimmerman, B.J. (2002). Achieving self-regulation: The trial and triumph of adolescence. In F. Pajares & T. Udan (Eds.), *Academic motivation of adolescents* (pp. 1–27). Greenwich, CT: Information Age.

Zimmerman, B.J., & Bandura, A. (1994). Impact of self-regulatory influences on writing course attainment. *American Educational Research Journal, 31,* 845–862.

Zimmerman, B.J., & Kitsantas, A. (1999). Acquiring writing revision skill: Shifting from process to outcome self-regulatory goals. *Journal of Educational Psychology, 91,* 1–10.

Zimmerman, B.J., & Martinez-Pons, M. (1990). Student differences in self-regulated learning: Relating grade, sex, and giftedness to self-efficacy and strategy use. *Journal of Educational Psychology, 82,* 51–59.

Index

Page numbers followed by *b*, *f*, and *t* indicate box, figure, and table, respectively.

Positive self-reaction, 106*b*
POSSE *see* Predict, organize, search, summarize, evaluate
Potential problems
  graphic organizers, 98–100, 100*t*
  prior knowledge, 57–58, 59–61
  questioning strategies, 78–81
  vocabulary, 44–45, 47–48
Poverty
  Matthew Effect and, 33*b*
  narrative text exposure and, 99
  school-based reading and, 117
Practical applications
  culturally relevant materials/ prior knowledge, 58*b*–59*b*
  oral proficiency/reading of English language learners (ELLs), 23*b*
  picture books to create shared background knowledge, 62*b*–63*b*
  scaffolded instruction in text structure, 89*b*–90*b*, 91*f*, 92*f*, 93*f*
  speech-language disorders/learning disabilities, 12*b*–13*b*
Pragmatics
  English language learners (ELLs) and, 15*b*
  overview of, 8–9
Predicates, 6–7
Predict, organize, search, summarize, evaluate (POSSE), 96
Prefixes
  morphological awareness and, 6
  vocabulary and, 37, 44
Previewing text features, 70, 71*f*
Print directionality, 5
Prior knowledge
  creating shared knowledge, 61–62, 62*b*–63*b*
  digging deeper, 52*b*
  English language learners (ELLs) and, 16, 57–58, 58*b*–59*b*, 60–61
  importance of instruction on, 51–52
  instructional techniques, 53–54, 53*f*, 54*f*, 55*f*, 56, 56*f*
  learning disabilities and, 11, 57, 61
  potential problems with, 57–58, 59–61
  practical applications, 58*b*–59*b*, 62*b*–63*b*
  questioning strategies and, 70
  vocabulary and, 45
Problem/solution text structure, 100*t*
Problem-solving processes, 104, 109*f*
Proficiency/reading level
  in English language learners (ELLs), 17*f*
  text selection and, 24, 26
Proposition/support text structure, 100*t*
Proverb about fishing, 110
Pyramids
  language and literacy, 4*f*
  views of reading instruction, 18–19, 18*f*

QAR *see* Question, Answer, Relationships
QRAC-the-Code (question, read, answer, check) strategy
  modeling example, 108*f*–109*f*
  overview of, 77*f*, 78
Question(s)
  content free, 88, 96–98
  relevance-fostering, 119
  rubrics for, 70, 72–73, 72f
  strategies using, *see* Questioning strategies
Question, Answer, Relationships (QAR), 68
Question, read, answer, check (QRAC-the-Code) strategy
  modeling example, 108*f*–109*f*
  overview of, 77*f*, 78
Question rubrics
  example, 72f
  guide for teaching, 72–73
  overview of, 70
Questioning strategies
  before/during/after reading, 68, 81
  for expository texts, 96–98
  importance of instruction on, 65
  instructional techniques for, 68–70, 69*f*, 71*f*, 72–73, 72*f*
  potential problems with, 78–81
  self-questioning, 107, 108*f*–109*f*
  summarizing text, 73, 74*f*, 75*f*, 76, 77*f*, 78
  types of questions, 66–68, 67*f*

RAP strategy, 76
Read 180 program, 25*f*
Readability levels
  evaluating, 27*t*
  of textbooks, 2
Readability Statistics, 27*t*
Readers (materials)
  culture and prior knowledge, 58*b*–59*b*
  interesting/meaningful, 28, 29*t*
Reading
  basic skills, *see* Basic reading skills
  daily, 32
  levels in English language learners (ELLs), 17*f*
Reading comprehension
  break down of, 21
  classroom implications, 18–19
  digging deeper, 5*b*, 10*b*–11*b*, 14*b*–15*b*
  dual diagnosis, 16, 18
  English language learners (ELLs) and, 13, 14*b*–15*b*, 15–16, 17*f*
  language development and, 4–9, 4*f*, 12*b*–13*b*
  learning disabilities and, 9, 10*b*–11*b*, 11–12, 12*b*–13*b*